The Whydah

A PIRATE SHIP FEARED, WRECKED, AND FOUND

MARTIN W. SANDLER

CANDLEWICK PRESS

First edition 2017

Library of Congress Catalog Card Number pending

ISBN 978-0-7636-8033-6

16 17 18 19 20 21 SHD 10 9 8 7 6 5 4 3 2 1

Printed in Ann Arbor, MI

This book was typeset in Adobe Caslon.

Candlewick Press
99 Dover Street
Somerville, Massachusetts 02144

visit us at www.candlewick.com

For Susan, Jill, Scott, Laura, and Craig
from a very proud father

Contents

Introduction

In 1984, newspaper headlines and television newscasts around the world announced that the wreck of the pirate ship *Whydah* had been discovered off Cape Cod. The *Whydah* was the first sunken pirate ship ever to be found. It had lain undiscovered for so long—almost three hundred years—that many had come to wonder if it had ever existed, if the incredible stories they had heard about the ship, its crew, and its amazing cargo of treasure were actually myths.

The stories connected with the *Whydah* are tales of pure adventure, populated by colorful characters, including one of the boldest and most successful pirates ever. Filled with outlandish deeds, amazing courage, barbarous acts, triumphs, and tragedy, the stories are made even more extraordinary by the fact that they are true.

The saga of the *Whydah* continued after it went down, and this part of its story is, in many ways, as fascinating as the tales of deeds and misdeeds aboard the ship when it rode the high seas. In the ordinary course of events, ships that outlive their usefulness are stripped or broken apart. But over the centuries, many have been shipwrecked—so many that much of human history lies hidden beneath the waves. Famed oceanographer Robert Ballard has described shipwrecks as "the pyramids of the deep." "I think there's more history in the deep," he has said, "than in all the museums in the world combined."

When a ship sinks, it becomes a time capsule. If it is salvaged, like the *Whydah,* it provides evidence of what ships were like and what life was like at the time of its sinking.

The *Whydah* was not only the first sunken pirate vessel to be discovered; it was also the first pirate ship to be excavated. Marine archaeologists have uncovered artifacts in its wreck that have changed our entire notion of who the pirates were and how they lived. Pirates have long been the subject of legend and literature—and considerable imagination. But the true story of the pirates is every bit as fascinating as the fiction they spawned.

Martin W. Sandler
Cotuit, Massachusetts

CHAPTER ONE

The Slave Ship Whydah

IN FEBRUARY 1717, Captain Lawrence Prince was heading home, back to England, on his ship the *Whydah,* which was loaded with a fortune in gold, silver, and other valuable goods. It was the final leg of the magnificent vessel's highly successful maiden voyage.

Formally named the *Whydah Gally,* the ship was built in 1715 for Sir Humphry Morice. A member of the British parliament, Morice was one of the most active slave traders of his day. His new ship, named for the infamous West African slave trading port Ouidah, was constructed to carry captured Africans to Caribbean plantations, where sugar, rice, tobacco, indigo, and other highly valued products were grown. There the captives would be sold into slavery.

Morice selected Lawrence Prince to be the ship's captain. It was an understandable choice, as Prince was well suited to command a ship constructed for such a brutal purpose. He had spent several years serving under the feared Welsh privateer Captain Henry Morgan, who had been employed by England to capture or destroy Spanish ships and raid Spanish towns in the Caribbean. That Prince could be ruthless in carrying out his duties is evidenced by an official Spanish government report of a raid he led on a town in Nicaragua. Prince, the report stated, "made havoc and a thousand destructions, sending the head of a priest in a basket and demanding 70,000 pesos in ransom."

In 1671, Prince helped lead Morgan's raid on Panama. His share of plunder from the attack allowed him to retire to Jamaica, where he lived as a prosperous landowner for more than forty years before being given command of the *Whydah*. It was an impressive ship. Three-masted and 102 feet long, it featured the most advanced nautical technology available, including state-of-the-art steering mechanisms and the most up-to-date navigational and sounding equipment. It was armed with eighteen cannons and had room for ten more. Extremely strong, the *Whydah* could carry three hundred tons of cargo. Most impressive of all, it was fast, capable of traveling over the waves at the then-amazing speed of just over thirteen knots, or fifteen miles per hour. Among the ship's most visible features was a long platform on its deck for captives who could not fit in the vessel's huge hold during the long voyage from Africa to the Americas. They would be shackled to the platform, lying side by side, exposed to all weather, with a barrier separating the male prisoners from the women and children, many of them their wives, sons, and daughters.

Early in 1716, with Captain Prince at its helm, the *Whydah* set sail from England loaded with cloth, firearms, gunpowder, liquor, hand tools, utensils, and other trade goods. The ship sailed along the coast of West Africa, passing what is today the Gambia, Senegal, and Nigeria, until it reached Ouidah, its namesake port. There Prince exchanged his cargo for almost four hundred slaves. The price Prince paid for each of the slaves is not known, but records from the Royal African Company, one of the world's largest traders in slaves, show that in 1731, the company bought forty slaves in Ouidah by trading 337 rifles, 40 muskets, and 530 pounds of gunpowder.

The *Whydah*'s voyage from England to West Africa was the first leg of the infamous slave-trading route known as the Triangular Trade. Once the four hundred slaves were crammed aboard his ship, Prince set sail across what was called the Middle Passage, headed for the Caribbean island of Jamaica. It was an almost ten-week voyage, during which nearly 20 percent of the captives died. The slavers did not provide enough food, and they packed their captives as tightly as possible. In these conditions, diseases such as smallpox, measles, and dysentery often spread out of control. Some of the slaves tried to commit suicide by throwing themselves overboard, but they were

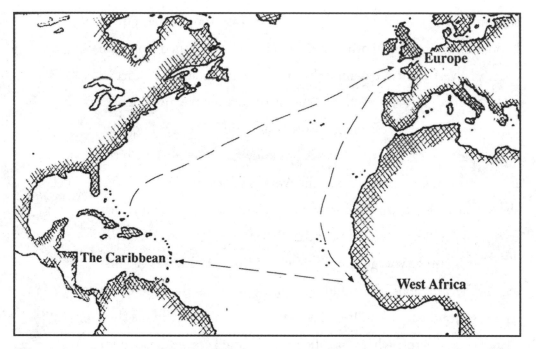

This map shows the route of the Triangular Trade in which ships sailed from England and other European countries to the coast of West Africa loaded with goods to exchange for slaves. The second leg of the journey brought the slaves from Africa to the Caribbean, where slave labor was used by plantation owners. The slaves were traded for gold, silver, and other valuables, which were shipped back to Europe for the final leg of the journey.

prevented from doing so by the special netting installed all around the deck. Despite their ordeal, 312 unfortunate souls survived and were dropped off at a huge Jamaican sugar plantation, where they were forced to work for the rest of their lives. Prince, on the other hand, received a fortune in gold, silver, and other valuables from the plantation owners to take home to the *Whydah*'s owners in exchange for having delivered his human cargo.

Prince was little concerned about the slaves' horrific plight. He would have focused on getting home as quickly and as safely as possible and being rewarded with the handsome payment he would surely receive. As the *Whydah* was proceeding in waters off the West Indies, two distant specks came into view. It soon became apparent that they were heading toward the *Whydah*. Could they be two friendly vessels, their captains anxious to exchange news and gossip with a fellow mariner? Could they be antislavery warships determined to capture or destroy vessels engaged in the slave trade? Or could they be pirates? This last possibility struck terror into the hearts of every ship owner and captain.

Prince and his crew had no way of knowing from this distance that the two specks were indeed pirate ships. Not only that, but they were commanded by a man who, in the space of just one year, had become one of the most feared pirate captains of his day.

The Evil Institution

SLAVERY DID NOT BEGIN in the Americas. What came to be called "the evil institution" existed in every ancient civilization, including Arabia, Greece, and the Roman Empire. The transportation of more than twelve million slaves from West Africa to Europe's American colonies, however, was one of the largest movement of slaves in history.

The Caribbean islands had everything needed for the establishment of a thriving plantation system: extensive open land, fertile soil, good harbors, and a climate perfectly suited to growing raw materials that were in demand throughout Europe. Everything, that is, except the enormous number of laborers needed to do the backbreaking work that growing and harvesting plantation crops required. The plantation owners found their answer in slave labor and made their fortunes on the backs of millions of captured African men, women, and children. The slave owners' continued prosperity was based on the labor of generations of captives who were born into slavery on their plantations.

Many of the millions of captives who were taken from Africa to the New World were kidnapped by African tribal chiefs and then sold to

British slave merchants called factors who lived in Africa. Others were taken prisoner in tribal wars started by these chiefs for the sole purpose of acquiring captives to be sold. The slave rosters also included those who had been convicted of crimes. In some cases, African chiefs fabricated crimes so that they could increase the number available to be sold into slavery.

Millions of others were captured by British slave traders who traveled inland to ambush and seize local men, women, and children. After being taken, these captives were chained in long lines called coffles and forced to walk as many as a thousand miles to the coast, where they were held, sometimes for as long as a year, in prisons called factories until a slave ship like the *Whydah* arrived.

People were kidnapped from all corners of Africa, from grasslands, farmlands, and cities such as Loango or Timbuktu, vital centers of scholarship and learning. They included the wealthy as well as the poor and artists whose work was highly valued throughout the world. Slavery is traumatic and dehumanizing, and the psychological damage Africans suffered when torn from their homes, families, native land, and everything else they cherished was as devastating as the physical pain and cruelty they would experience once transported and sold.

An unspeakable tragedy for millions, being enslaved was eloquently

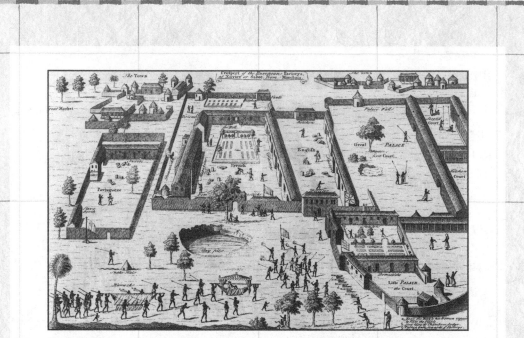

Various European countries that were engaged in the slave trade maintained compounds in Africa, where captives were held until ships arrived to transport them to the Americas. The compounds shown here, in what is now Nigeria, belonged to England, France, Portugal, and the Netherlands.

described by one of the very few slaves to leave behind an account of his feelings and experiences, Ghana native Quobna Ottobah Cugoano: "It would be needless," he wrote, "to give a description of all the horrible scenes which we saw, and the base treatment which we met with in this dreadful captive situation. . . . Let it suffice to say, that I was thus lost to my dear indulgent parents and relations, and they to me. . . . Brought from a state of innocence and freedom, and, in a barbarous and cruel manner, conveyed to a state of horror and slavery."

CHAPTER TWO

A New Pirate King

HIS NAME WAS SAMUEL BELLAMY. He was sometimes called Black Sam or Black Bellamy because of his jet-black hair and dark complexion. And he didn't wear his hair under a powdered wig, as was the fashion of the time, but grew it long and tied it back with a black satin bow. With his long velvet coat, knee britches, silk stockings, and silver-buckled shoes, he cut a most dashing figure. His outfit was completed by the sword that hung at his left hip and the four pistols that were secured by a broad sash. Even though he could be as ferocious, and even as brutal, as any of his fellow pirate leaders, he often showed mercy and generosity toward those whom he captured on his raids. These traits earned him the nickname Robin Hood of the Seas.

Bellamy was born in the winter of 1689 in a small town near the seafaring city of Plymouth, England. The sea was in his blood, and he became a sailor on some of his neighbors' boats even before he reached his teens. He was still not twenty when he joined the

British navy and took part in several battles in the War of Spanish Succession, a conflict involving the major powers of Europe, including England. When the war ended in 1714, Great Britain abruptly released more than forty thousand sailors from service. Among those newly unemployed was twenty-four-year-old Sam Bellamy, who decided to seek his fortune in America.

He arrived in Provincetown, on the tip of Cape Cod, in the spring of 1715. The following spring, in nearby Newport, Rhode Island, he met Paulsgrave Williams. The two were destined to become best friends and fellow adventurers. Forty-two-year-old Williams, whose father had been attorney general of Rhode Island, came from a wealthy family. He had also become well off in his own right by establishing himself as a highly successful goldsmith. But, like Sam Bellamy, Williams was dissatisfied with his life. He wanted adventure. Bellamy, too, sought adventure, but more than anything else, he wanted to be rich.

For more than a hundred years, Spanish ships called galleons had been transporting enormous amounts of gold, silver, jewels, and other treasures mined in the New World or stolen from the native peoples who lived there. Over these years, a good number of galleons had been lost at sea, the victims of hurricanes, typhoons, and other disasters. Stories of these sunken treasure ships had fired the imaginations of adventurers on both sides of the Atlantic who were eager to get their hands on the lost riches. Sam Bellamy was one of these men. And he had a particular treasure in mind.

On July 30, 1715, not long after Bellamy arrived in Provincetown, eleven Spanish ships loaded with tons of gold and silver sank off the coast of Florida in a hurricane. All this treasure was still lying on the seabed a year later. Here was their golden chance, Bellamy told Williams, their chance to get rich beyond their wildest dreams, their chance to live like kings. What they needed to do was get to the spot where the ships had gone down and bring up the treasure before the Spanish mounted a recovery effort. Williams needed no convincing, and he promised Bellamy that he would lend him the money to buy a ship and hire a crew to make the dream a reality.

According to legend, Sam Bellamy met someone else in the late spring of 1716 who would have a profound influence on his life. While Paulsgrave Williams was raising the money to finance their treasure-seeking adventure, Bellamy was living at Higgins Tavern in the Cape Cod town of Eastham. One warm June evening, he took a walk through the cemetery adjoining the tavern. He had just begun his stroll when he heard the sound of a young woman singing. He came upon an apple tree, and sitting under it, absorbed in her song, was a young woman with the most golden hair and the deepest blue eyes he had ever seen. He could go no farther. He had to get to know that girl.

Bellamy introduced himself. He learned that her name was Maria Hallett and that she was fifteen years old. He told her what it was like to serve in the British navy, what the battles at sea were like, and how much he wanted to make a success of himself.

For her part, Maria had never seen a man as lively and as handsome as Sam Bellamy. And there was something more. Strange as it might seem to draw such a conclusion in just one meeting, there was no doubt about it: something in his eyes told her that he indeed was going to make a name for himself.

From their first meeting until Bellamy left in search of the Spanish treasure, he and Maria spent as much time together as they possibly could. But there was a problem. Maria's parents were not pleased with what was obviously developing into a serious relationship. As prosperous farmers, they had far more ambitious plans for their young daughter than a life with a sailor who, as far as they could tell, had little chance of providing Maria with the comforts they wished for her.

Still, Maria kept up her relationship with Bellamy. Her feelings for him grew even stronger when he told her about the Spanish wrecks. He assured her that her parents would greet him with open arms when he returned to the Cape with a ship loaded with gold, silver, and precious jewels. As for her, he stated, he had every intention of marrying her when he returned and then taking her to the Caribbean and making her princess of their own island.

Almost everything in the remarkable story of Sam Bellamy is well documented. Everything, that is, except the tale of Maria Hallett. As authors Barry Clifford and Paul Perry wrote, "The truth about [Sam and Maria's] brief relationship will always remain shrouded in speculation." But as author Arthur T. Vanderbilt has also written, "I would not be surprised if, someday, someone came across musty old records that prove there was a fifteen-year-old girl named Maria Hallett who lived on the outer Cape in 1716, and there met the young sailor with dreams of Spanish gold."

What is certain is that in early 1716, Bellamy, Williams, and a crew of about thirty men, including skilled divers, left Cape Cod in a small ship that Williams had obtained and sailed to the site of the wreck of the Spanish treasure fleet. When they arrived, they were hardly alone. Other groups of divers were attempting to locate the treasure as well. And no one was finding anything.

For the next full month, the fortune seekers kept at it, sending their divers down to every likely spot. Finally, their provisions ran out. So, too, did their hopes. They hadn't found a single silver bar or one gold coin. Eventually they would learn that they hadn't beaten the Spanish government to it after all: Spain had already completed a salvage operation so large and so successful that almost 80 percent of the treasure had been recovered. The remainder of the bounty would not be found for another 250 years, by treasure hunters working with advanced modern equipment.

In the meantime, Sam Bellamy was devastated. Gone were his dreams of instant wealth. He was embarrassed as well. He had boasted to people throughout Cape Cod that he would return with enormous riches. The thought of coming back empty-handed was something that neither he nor Paulsgrave Williams could bear.

More than ever, Bellamy was desperate to succeed. And out of that desperation came a bold plan. If he couldn't find treasure underneath the sea, then he would seize it from ships sailing on the surface. He would, in the language of the day, go "on the account." He would become a pirate.

Bellamy certainly had the heart of a pirate. Although he could be compassionate, he could also be ruthless. There was no question that he was brave and adventurous. Paulsgrave Williams was ready to join him, as were the thirty members of his treasure-seeking crew, all of whom were also bitterly disappointed at not having gained a share of sunken Spanish treasure. Prior to asking them to vote on whether or not they wanted to join his pirate band, Bellamy stood in front of them holding a pirate flag. "This flag," he told them, "represents not death, but resurrection. . . . From this day, we are new men."

As their captain, Bellamy traded their salvage boat for two pirogues, huge flat-bottom sailing canoes large enough to carry at least fifty men and several powerful swivel guns. The sight of two vessels with their occupants shouting wildly, waving their cutlasses, and arming their swivel guns became one of the most frightening sights the crew of any merchant vessel could see. Bellamy was so successful at raiding ships this way that before long, he became the talk of the pirate community.

Among those impressed with the reports of Bellamy's raids was one of the most influential pirates of them all. His name was Benjamin Hornigold and he was a living legend, not only because of the amazing number of vessels he had captured and plundered but also for the number of successful pirate captains and officers he had trained. Among his protégés at that time was a renegade named Edward Teach, who, under the name Blackbeard, would eventually become arguably the most famous pirate of all.

Always on the lookout for more pirate talent, Hornigold met with Bellamy and invited him, Williams, and their crew to join his band. Bellamy was thrilled. Only months before, having failed to find the sunken treasure he had been dreaming about for so long,

Although his reign of terror lasted little more than two years, the man known as Blackbeard was the most feared pirate ever to sail the seas. To terrorize his victims, Blackbeard would weave matches into his hair and beard and then ignite them before going into battle.

he had been tempted to regard himself a failure. Now not only was he a budding pirate star, but he was also about to sail with Ben Hornigold aboard his flagship the *Marianne* and alongside the *Postillion* and its famous captain Olivier LeBous, who often prowled the Caribbean with Hornigold in search of prey.

Bellamy and his men had been aboard the *Marianne* a short time when Hornigold and LeBous took their ships on an extended voyage throughout the Caribbean, successfully pillaging merchant ships, particularly in the waters around Cuba. Late in May 1716, they sailed to the island of Hispaniola and anchored in a large bay. There a dispute that had been simmering for some time broke out among Hornigold's sailors. As the *Marianne* had been sailing around Cuba, its lookouts had spotted several British merchant vessels, but Hornigold had refused to go after them. Proud of his English roots, he had developed a policy of not robbing British ships, no matter how valuable a cargo they might be carrying.

That was a policy that most of Hornigold's crew could not abide. To them, every ship was fair game, and the greatest crime of all was letting a ship filled with treasure escape their grasp. When the *Marianne* anchored in Hispaniola, the crew voted to oust Hornigold as their captain. Abiding by the pirate code under which they operated, Hornigold and twenty-six men loyal to him accepted the vote, left the *Marianne,* and sailed off in a ship that

The Articles of Agreement

LIFE ABOARD A PIRATE SHIP was governed by a code of laws called the Articles of Agreement, or simply the Articles, which were developed in the last half of the 1600s by pirates in the West Indies. No one could become a full-fledged member of a pirate crew unless he went on the account, meaning he first signed the Articles of Agreement and then swore on a Bible, an ax, or a skull to obey them. The *Whydah's* copy of the Articles was not recovered, but Bellamy's crew would have been governed by rules much like these, from the notorious pirate Captain Bartholomew Roberts:

I. Every man shall have an equal vote in affairs of moment. He shall have an equal title to fresh provisions or strong liquors at any time seized, and shall use them at pleasure unless a scarcity may make it necessary for the common good that a retrenchment may be voted.

II. Every man shall be called fairly in turn by the list on board of prizes. But if they defraud the company to the value of even a Piece of Eight in plate, jewels or money, they shall be marooned. If any man rob another he shall have his nose and ears slit and be put ashore where he shall be sure to encounter hardships.

III.   None shall game for money either with dice or cards.

IV.   The lights and candles should be put out at eight at night, and if any of the crew desire to drink after that hour they shall sit upon the open deck without lights.

V.   Each man shall keep his piece, cutlass and pistols at all times clean and ready for action.

VI.   No boy or woman to be allowed amongst them. If any man shall be found seducing any of the latter sex and carrying her to sea in disguise he shall suffer death.

VII.   He that shall desert the ship or his quarters in time of battle shall be punished by death or marooning.

VIII.   None shall strike another on board the ship, but every man's quarrel shall be ended on shore by sword or pistol in this manner. At the word of command from the quartermaster, each man being previously placed back to back, shall turn and fire immediately. If any man do not, the quartermaster shall knock the piece out of his hand. If both miss their aim they shall take to their cutlasses, and he that draweth first blood shall be declared the victor.

IX. No man shall talk of breaking up their way of living till each has a share of 1,000 [pounds]. Every man who shall become a cripple or lose a limb in his service shall have 800 pieces of eight from common stock and for lesser hurts proportionately.

X. The captain and the quartermaster shall receive two shares of a prize, the master gunner and boatswain, one and one half shares, all other officers one and one quarter, and private gentlemen of fortune one share each.

XI. The musicians shall have rest on the Sabbath Day only by right. On all other days by favour only.

was part of Hornigold's flotilla. In the short time that Bellamy had been aboard the *Marianne,* he must have impressed the crew, for as soon as Hornigold and his followers, including Blackbeard, departed, the rest of the crew voted Sam Bellamy to be their new captain.

It was the beginning of what was probably the most amazing single year of capture and plunder in the long history of piracy. Bellamy, Williams, and their men quickly became the most feared pirates the Caribbean and the Atlantic had ever witnessed. They chased, stopped, and boarded every merchant ship they spotted. The sailors in these vessels put up very little resistance. They were terrified simply by the sight of pirates. Besides, they weren't being paid nearly enough to risk their lives defending goods that didn't belong to them.

After the booty was removed from each ship he captured, Bellamy usually let the prize vessel move on, but not before offering the sailors on the plundered ship the chance to join his pirate crew. Sometimes, however, Bellamy would spot one of the merchant seamen who had a special skill that he felt was needed on his ship. That man would be forced to join the pirate crew, whether he wanted to or not.

As he had done with Ben Hornigold, Olivier LeBous in the *Postillion* often partnered with Bellamy. On November 9, 1716,

A Barbarous Calling

PIRATES WERE NOT the likable rogues portrayed in popular books and the movies. What has been referred to as the golden age of piracy was in fact "a period of unrestrained murder, robbery, and kidnapping on the high seas." True stories of pirate cruelty shocked the populace throughout the 1700s. Among the most widely circulated tale was that of a captured merchant captain whose incessant talking so annoyed his pirate captors that they sewed his lips together with an enormous needle usually used to repair sails. Another defeated captain and his crew were sewn up in a sail and thrown overboard. When the sail washed ashore, twenty-eight bodies were found inside.

Many of the pirates' cruelest acts, including those of the men of the *Whydah*, were carried out against crews who refused to surrender immediately. Other brutalities were aimed at forcing a merchant vessel's captain and crew to reveal where their most valuable cargo was hidden. And records, including those of the *Whydah*, reveal that some pirates acted cruelly simply because it was in their nature.

Over the years, pirates developed an arsenal of brutalities. One of their favorite tactics was called sweating, in which they forced their victim to run around and around the mainmast while they threw broken bottles at him and jabbed him with pointed tools or weapons.

Another favorite was described by English captain William Snelgrave. While being held captive on a pirate ship, he looked on in horror as the pirates abused a French captain who had refused to surrender when first fired upon. They "put a Rope about his Neck," wrote Snelgrave, "and hoisted him up and down several times to the Main-yard-arm till he was almost dead." The French captain was actually lucky. On some occasions, when the victim survived hoisting, he was shot to death.

It was a brutal business, and among the cruelest was pirate Edward "Ned" Low. Described by his own men as a "maniac and a brute," on one occasion, he had a merchant ship's captain and his entire thirty-two-man crew killed because the captain dropped a bag of gold into the sea rather than turning it over to Low. His own crew finally set Low adrift in an open boat without food or water. A French ship rescued him, but when they recognized him, they gave him a brief trial and then hanged him.

No account of pirate cruelty would be complete without invoking the name of Blackbeard. Sam Bellamy's onetime shipmate and arguably the fiercest pirate captain of them all once interrupted a friendly game of cards to shoot his first mate for no apparent reason. Asked why, Blackbeard replied that if he didn't shoot one or two of his crewmen now and then, they'd forget who he was.

after capturing and looting several small vessels off the Virgin Islands, they came upon a major prize. Between the islands of St. Thomas and what is now St. Croix, the lookouts on both the *Marianne* and the *Postillion* spotted a large English merchant ship. It was the *Bonetta*, carrying a huge cargo from Jamaica to Antigua. The two pirate vessels gave chase, and when they got close to the *Bonetta*, LeBous raised a pirate flag, complete with skull and crossbones. Bellamy fired a cannon shot across the prize vessel's bow. Captain Savage of the *Bonetta* needed no more convincing. Not even waiting for a boarding party to appear, he had some of his men row him over to the *Marianne*, where he formally surrendered himself and his ship to Bellamy.

The *Bonetta*'s cargo was so large that Bellamy ordered Captain Savage to anchor the ship off St. Croix, where the *Marianne* and the *Postillion* joined them. For the better part of two weeks, while Savage and his crew were held prisoner on the island, the men of the two pirate ships transferred the captured goods from the *Bonetta*'s hold to their vessels.

When the transfer was finally completed and Bellamy was about to let Savage sail away with his empty ship, he made his usual offer to the *Bonetta*'s crew. Any sailor who wanted to become a pirate and join the *Marianne*'s crew was invited to do so. What happened next totally surprised Bellamy and his men. Stepping forward to accept the offer was John King, who, with his mother, was a passenger on board the *Bonetta*.

It might not have been surprising that a passenger on a seagoing vessel would, for whatever reason, welcome the chance to become a pirate. But John King was at most ten years old. Young as he was, after watching Bellamy and his men in action, he was determined to join the pirates. Understandably, King's mother became hysterical at the thought. But John King was so determined to become a pirate that he first threatened to kill himself and then threatened to kill his mother if he was not allowed to join Bellamy's crew. As for Bellamy, he could not help but admire King's determination, and John King became not only the youngest member of Bellamy's crew but also the youngest pirate ever known.

Bellamy was ready to sail on. He told Captain Savage that he was now free to sail away with the *Bonetta* as well. For Savage, being held captive for two weeks by Bellamy had been an extraordinary experience. During that time he had looked on in amazement as Bellamy and his men, despite being in the middle of looting the *Bonetta*, had chased, captured, plundered, and then released a French merchant ship and six smaller vessels. What Savage also remembered vividly was Bellamy telling him that his greatest wish was to capture a vessel even bigger than the *Marianne* so that he and his men could travel faster and farther in their quest to rule the seas.

In December 1716, Bellamy got his wish. As he and LeBous were sailing the waters near Saba, a tiny, five-square-mile island off the Virgin Islands, they captured two ships, the *Pearl* and the *Sultana*. To Bellamy's delight, the *Sultana* was the type of ship that he was looking for to replace the *Marianne* as his flagship. After looting the *Pearl* and forcing several men from the *Sultana* to join his crew, Black Sam told Captain Tosor of the *Pearl* that he was free to sail away with his crew and the rest of the men from the *Sultana*. Then he transferred his own crew to his new flagship and handed over command of the *Marianne* to Paulsgrave Williams.

CHAPTER THREE

Bigger Ships, Bigger Prizes

IT DID NOT TAKE LONG for Bellamy to establish the *Sultana* as one of the most feared of pirate vessels. On December 16, 1716, just a day after taking command of his new flagship, he and LeBous, with Williams and the *Marianne* also operating in the vicinity, captured a merchant ship out of Bristol, England, called the *St. Michael.* They held the ship's crew on the nearby island of St. Maarten while they plundered its cargo. They then returned the ship to its captain, but not before thirteen of his crew voluntarily joined the men of the *Sultana.* A fourteenth member of the *St. Michael*'s crew also became part of Bellamy's pirate band, but his participation was anything but voluntary.

His name was Thomas Davis. Having first gone to sea when he was seventeen, he was now the *St. Michael*'s shipwright, or onboard carpenter. The last thing Davis wanted was to be a pirate, but the *Sultana* badly needed his skills. As Bellamy ordered Davis aboard the *Sultana,* the young man begged him to let him go. The *St. Michael*'s captain also pleaded for Davis's release. Finally, even

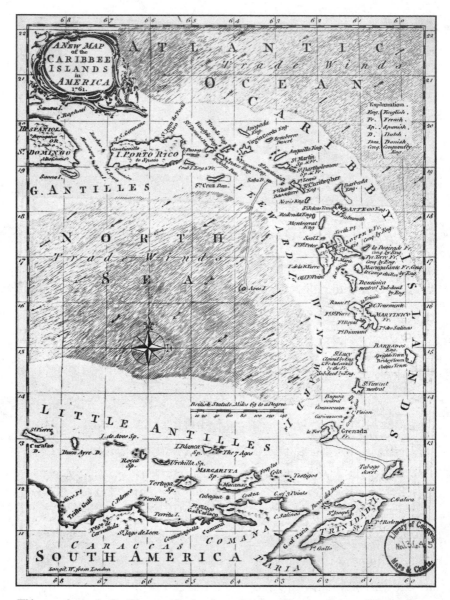

This map shows the Caribbean at the time known as the golden age of piracy. Because of its location between the southern tip of North America and the northern part of South America, the Caribbean contained major trade routes for merchant ships, making it prime hunting grounds for pirate ships constantly on the prowl.

though he had promised the carpenter that he would eventually be set free, Bellamy called a meeting of the pirates and let them decide Davis's fate. The crew, offended by the fact that he had so vehemently opposed becoming a pirate, forced Davis to do just that.

The *St. Michael* would rank as one of the largest vessels Bellamy plundered after he took command of the *Sultana*. It was the first ship he took using a strategy that would become known throughout the seafaring world. As soon as they spotted prey, Williams, in the fast, highly maneuverable *Marianne*, would chase after it and track it down. Just as the targeted ship was preparing to put up a fight, Bellamy would show up in the much larger *Sultana*, its cannons pointing ominously at the prize vessel. On almost every occasion, the result would be an immediate surrender.

As Bellamy became increasingly successful and well known, LeBous grew tired of operating in the younger pirate's shadow. By mutual agreement, they parted ways, and LeBous sailed off to seek glory of his own. Bellamy, on the other hand, now had a different desire. The *Sultana*'s hold was filled almost to capacity with barrels and crates containing clothing, cloth, foodstuffs, and other valuable plundered goods. Special compartments that had been built in the space between the deck and the hold housed bags of coins, gold dust, and jewelry. The exact value of the stolen treasure on the *Sultana* was not recorded, but there is no question that it was worth a significant fortune. Yet Bellamy was not satisfied. He wanted an even bigger, faster ship, one that could carry even more booty, one that could outrun even the British navy's fastest ships.

Then, in late February 1717, the *Sultana*'s lookout spotted the *Whydah* making its way back to England. As Bellamy gazed out at the huge slave ship, he realized he was looking at his heart's desire. Like some other pirate captains, Bellamy craved having a slave vessel for his flagship. Slave ships were built for speed so that they could complete the Middle Passage as quickly as possible, and they were also larger than most other vessels. Speed and size were important assets to pirate ships for pursuing prey and for storing large amounts of plunder. And slave ships had two other valuable features as well: they were always heavily armed, and they had huge kitchens called galleys, with large cooking pots and other utensils that could be used to feed more than a hundred men.

Now, as Williams trailed behind him in the *Marianne*, Bellamy stepped up his pursuit in a race that under ordinary circumstances the far swifter *Whydah* would have easily won. Bellamy could not have known it, but his chase was aided by an extraordinarily valuable cargo whose equally extraordinary weight slowed his target.

Still, it took Bellamy's vessel three full days of sailing as fast as it could through the waters between Cuba and Hispaniola, known as the Windward Passage, to catch up with Captain Prince's expertly piloted ship. Finally, the *Sultana* pulled within cannon range of the slave vessel off Long Island, in the Bahamas. Bellamy had already ordered that his personal pirate flag be raised. Now he had his gunners fire two shots across the *Whydah*'s bow. The experienced Captain Prince, fully aware that to put up a fight he had no chance of winning meant incurring brutal treatment at the hands of the pirates, lowered both the *Whydah*'s flag and its sails, indicating his official surrender.

Once Prince gave in, Bellamy ordered that he anchor the *Whydah* off Long Island and, within hours, began the task of transferring his huge cargo of booty from the *Sultana* to the *Whydah*. The transfer took several days and was a remarkable sight: there, in a remote area of the vast Caribbean, small boats continually traveled back and forth between the two ships, accompanied by shouts from Bellamy and his officers directing where on the *Whydah* the crew members should place the *Sultana*'s cargo.

Bellamy and his men always looked forward to discovering what was included in the loot they had just captured. But when they looked in the *Whydah*'s hold and between its decks, they received the greatest and happiest surprise of their lives.

In the *Whydah*'s hold, the pirates found hundreds of elephant tusks stacked like cordwood, representing a fortune in ivory alone. Slabs of cinchona, bark used for making quinine, a medicine for

The Jolly Roger

SAM BELLAMY well knew what he was doing when he raised his personal flag as soon as he got close to the *Whydah*. In the first decades of the 1700s, nothing terrified the captain and crew of a merchant vessel more than the sight of a pirate flag flying from the mast of an approaching ship. Known as a Jolly Roger no matter what its design, the flag let the captain of the ship being attacked know that he was facing one of the most important decisions of his life — to surrender immediately or to try to fight off the pirate attackers.

No one knows the origin of the pirate flag. It probably dates back to the days when a ship attacking another vessel would fly a plain black flag to convey the message that if the other ship surrendered at once, no harm would come to the captured crew. If the vessel under attack refused to give in immediately, the attacking ship raised a plain red flag to show that no mercy would be given.

There is no consensus either as to where the name Jolly Roger came from. Some historians believe that it originated in the 1600s when some French mariners began calling the red flag *le joli rouge*, or "pretty red"

in French. Other pirate historians believe it originated in
English, as in the 1600s "roger"
was a term for a vagabond or
a vagrant, and "Jolly Roger"
referred to the vagabonds of
the sea. Still others tie it to
the early-seventeenth-century
term "old Roger" as a name
for the Devil and believe that a
Jolly Roger flag sent the message that anyone who resisted
the pirates would incur the
wrath of the Devil.

Beginning in the late
1600s, reputation-conscious

This illustration from Daniel Defoe's General History
of the Robberies and Murders of the Most Notorious
Pyrates, *published in 1724, shows the pirate Stede
Bonnet gazing out at his ship, which is flying a Jolly
Roger. Bonnet, unlike almost all other pirates, came
from a wealthy family and went on the account not
for money but for the sheer adventure of it.*

pirate captains, intent on having everyone know exactly who they were,
began to personalize their flags by adding symbols. Common symbols
were skeletons, daggers, and cutlasses, all meant to convey death to those
who did not surrender immediately. A pierced heart warned that no mercy
would be shown to anyone who resisted. An hourglass meant that time

was running out for the victims. Even more common than these symbols, however, was a skull with crossed bones beneath it.

The skull and crossed bones were so popular that they became the symbol with which pirates are associated to this day. Some pirate flags, however, suggest that their captains considered the skull and crossbones much too simple a design. Blackbeard flew a flag incorporating not one but several of the common symbols: a skeleton holding an hourglass, as well as a human heart impaled on a spear. The skeleton, as it was on other pirate flags, is horned, signifying that it is in league with the Devil.

Captain Bartholomew "Black Bart" Roberts provided a powerful example of how effective individual pirate flags could be. In June 1720, Black Bart sailed into the harbor at Trepassey, Newfoundland. He was flying his distinctive flag, which bore the image of a pirate and a spear-holding skeleton clutching an hourglass between them. Although he had no idea that there were twenty-two ships anchored at Trepassey, as soon as his flag was spotted, the crews of all twenty-two vessels abandoned their ships and fled in panic.

curing malaria, were also worth an enormous amount of money. Huge sacks and barrels of valuable sugar, molasses, and indigo plants for making dye filled the rest of the hold.

And between the *Whydah*'s decks were sacks and sacks of precious gold and silver. Also hidden were rare pieces of African jewelry and bags of gold dust. Most spectacular of all was a magnificent box of East Indian jewels, whose contents, according to one of the pirates, included a ruby the size of a hen's egg. As Peter Cornelius Hoof, a longtime Bellamy crew member, testified, "The Money taken in the [*Whydah*], which was reported to Amount to 20000 or 30000 Pounds, was counted over in the cabin, and put up in bags, Fifty Pounds to every Man's share, there being 180 Men on Board." When distributed, that was enough money to last most pirates a lifetime.

When all of the booty had been transferred, Bellamy, as was his custom, gave Captain Prince's crew the option of joining the pirates. A dozen men accepted the offer. At the same time, the young reluctant carpenter Thomas Davis reminded Bellamy that he had been promised eventual release. But once again the crew outvoted their captain's proposal to release the carpenter, with one pirate exclaiming that they "would first shoot him or whip him to Death at the Mast" before letting him leave.

The only question remaining was what to do with Captain Prince and the loyal members of his crew. Bellamy was grateful to Prince for surrendering so peacefully, keeping the *Whydah* and its extraordinary cargo from jeopardy. Black Sam was overjoyed to have acquired his ideal flagship and a booty far beyond anything he had ever imagined. So it was no surprise that he gave Prince the *Sultana* and told him that he and his crew were free to go.

They were no sooner out of sight than Bellamy began making physical changes to the *Whydah*. First, he had his crew remove the long platform on top of the pilot's cabin upon which many slaves had made the horrific journey from Africa to the Caribbean. Then, in order to make the *Whydah* even faster, they took down the forecastle, a structure in the ship's bow, where some of the slave ship's crew had been quartered. It was tall and bulky and its weight reduced the maximum speed the *Whydah* could attain. So, too, did the pilot's cabin and the quarterdeck, a raised deck behind the mainmast, both of which were also removed. Bellamy also had his men strip off the lead sheathing that covered the ship's hull and was designed to protect the vessel in the event of a collision with another ship. Bellamy hated to see it go, but he knew the *Whydah* was quicker and more maneuverable without it, and he felt it was a sacrifice he needed to make.

In addition, ten cannons were added to the ship, giving it twenty-eight large guns in all, an amazing number for a nonmilitary vessel. The *Whydah*'s dramatic transformation from a slave ship to one of the most formidable and speedy pirate vessels in history was complete.

CHAPTER FOUR

The Pirate Ship Whydah

THE **WHYDAH** had always been an extraordinary vessel. Now it was being manned by an extraordinary crew. They had gone on the account for the same reasons that almost all pirates in the late 1600s and the first decades of the 1700s had done so: a lack of better options. Europe was ruled by tyrannical kings and queens whose word was law. Ordinary people had no say in how things were done. More than half of the populations of countries like England were desperately poor—so poor that children as young as five were forced to work, usually in mining or manufacturing.

In desperation, many men chose to attempt to earn a living at sea on naval vessels or merchant ships. Most learned that it was an even harsher life than the one they had experienced on land. Some sea captains and their officers were sadistic individuals who delighted in inflicting the cruelest punishments imaginable on their crews. One of their favorite punishment methods was keelhauling, which entailed tying the sailor to a line looped under the ship, throwing him overboard, and hauling him from one side to the other, along the barnacle-encrusted hull, resulting in injuries and sometimes drowning.

The most common and most feared form of punishment, however, was flogging. Sailors were brutally beaten with a whip made of nine knotted ropes called a cat-o'-nine tails. British naval captains in particular did not hesitate to dole out up to one hundred lashes. Official records reveal that English sailors were flogged to death for crimes as minor as being late for an assignment or losing an oar. When their ships were captured by pirates, many sailors were all too willing to abandon the captains and officers who had treated them so cruelly, including feeding them rotten and worm-infested food, and join the pirates.

Escaping the horrendous conditions on merchant ships was not, however, the main reason that men became pirates. For many, the biggest reason to turn to piracy was the desire to be free men—to belong to no nation, to no master, to no one but themselves. Pirate historian Ken Kinkor put it this way: "Many would have seen the pirates as scoundrels pure and simple. I take a different approach. . . . If we look at the pattern of European society of the period, we are compelled to conclude that these men were not simple robbers, rather they were acting rightly or wrongly against social grievances." In Kinkor's view, pirates were "a subculture held together by a common spirit of revolt." Whether it was in the person of a king or a queen, or a merchant ship captain or a naval officer, pirates hated authority.

Aside from their desire to be free of authority, many sailors were drawn to piracy by the lure of money. An English seaman in the early 1700s was paid about 1 pound sterling a month ($200 in today's money), hardly enough to get by on. When they left the sea, they could not expect to earn much more on land. Piracy could change their fortunes dramatically. Each man on a pirate vessel received at least one share of the ship's plunder. In the late 1600s and the first decades of the 1700s, many pirate ships returned with booty plentiful enough that one share of it amounted to double the annual income of most London bankers and merchants—and equal to the annual income of many of the wealthiest people in England. It was, in fact, enough to allow a pirate to retire in comfort if he chose.

Historical documents indicate that pirate ships were the only vessels on which men of color were treated as equal members of the crew, and although records vary, it is safe to say that as many as fifty black crewmen served aboard the *Whydah*. Although the *Whydah* and other ships taken by Bellamy had transported slaves, nothing in the records indicates that his black crew had been on those ships as slaves. Most likely they were free blacks who fully understood how fortunate they were to be on a ship like the *Whydah,* one of the few places at sea or ashore where black men and white men were treated equally.

The ranks of the many men and a few women who in the 1600s and early 1700s became pirates included people from many different walks of life. Some were indentured servants who had run away; others were prisoners of war who had somehow managed to escape from the ship that was carrying them when it put into port; still others were young men looking for adventure. A large number of sailors, like Sam Bellamy, became pirates when they were released by the navy after the long War of the Spanish Succession. As a government official in the Bahamas proclaimed, "War is no sooner ended but the West Indies always swarms with pirates."

As much as they cherished being free spirits, pirates recognized that for a pirate ship to function effectively, it had to have a command structure. The *Whydah* was no exception. At the top was the captain. Among his many jobs was that of inspiring his men to perform to the best of their abilities and to never lose heart, particularly when the going got the toughest. He was also responsible for recruiting men from the ships he captured who could perform specific duties on his ship. To do this took an eloquent speaker, and there was no more eloquent or persuasive pirate captain than Black Sam Bellamy.

The second-in-command on a pirate vessel, the man on whom every pirate captain most relied, was the quartermaster. Like the captain, he was voted in by the crew and could be voted out at any time. The quartermaster was in charge of the day-to-day operations of the ship, and it was his responsibility to see that the captain's orders were carried out. It was also up to him to settle any disputes that arose between members of the crew.

The quartermaster also had responsibilities during a raid. He was the first to board prize ships. He chose the plunder that was to be taken and what was to be left behind. And he decided how the booty was to be divided among the crew, while obeying the guidelines established by the Articles of Agreement.

In addition, the quartermaster was responsible for punishing crew members for offenses large and small. Minor offenses included quarreling, abusing prisoners, and failing to keep one's weapons clean. The most serious crimes included disobeying the captain's orders, stealing from the crew, abandoning one's post in battle, deserting the ship, and murdering a fellow pirate. While the quartermaster immediately shot any deserter who was caught, those who were charged with other serious offenses were tried by their fellow pirates, who, on finding a crewmate guilty, determined the punishment to be carried out by the quartermaster.

Those convicted of serious offenses faced the same harsh treatment that so many of them had experienced in their past lives as merchant seamen or members of the navy, including flogging and keelhauling. The most brutal punishment was marooning. The disgraced pirate was placed on a deserted island and then abandoned without food, water, or shelter. All he was given was a pistol with which, if he preferred, he could kill himself before starving to death.

The *Whydah*'s quartermaster, Richard Noland, was a man perfectly suited for the job. He had begun his pirate career by sailing from his Irish homeland with Captain Ben Hornigold and had learned many of the pirate ways from that master teacher. He had an even temper, an eye for detail, and the ability to persuade others to do what he believed needed to be done — all important qualities for a quartermaster. Unlike most pirates, Noland could read and write and add and subtract — important skills for keeping track of and distributing the plunder.

Like the quartermaster, the boatswain was elected by the crew. He was in charge of keeping the ship in shape for travel or battle. Specifically, he made sure that the canvas, lines, and wood throughout the ship were in perfect condition and properly maintained. He supervised the crew as they set and lowered the sails; worked in the ropes, called rigging, that controlled the sails high above the deck; and lowered and raised the anchors. The boatswain also led parties ashore when supplies were needed.

The *Whydah*'s boatswain was another Irishman, Jeremiah Burke. One of the most experienced mariners on board, Burke had more than thirty years at sea, giving him the confidence necessary to effectively supervise the crew.

Along with Noland and Burke, Sam Bellamy counted himself lucky to have Englishman John Lambert aboard as sailing master, or navigator. During the golden age of piracy, navigational instruments were still primitive. Trained navigators and accurate sailing charts were rare. Lambert was skilled at navigating by the stars, and when the *Whydah* counted accurate sailing maps and charts among the booty it took from captured vessels, Lambert had the skills needed to read them and use them to the *Whydah*'s advantage. The *Whydah*'s pilot, a Miskito Indian named John Julian, was responsible for helping Lambert navigate through particularly unfamiliar waters. Julian was one of the first and also one of the youngest pirates that Bellamy recruited. Records of his birthplace are contradictory. Some state that he was born in either Honduras or Nicaragua, both home to the Miskito people. Others refer to him as "an Indian born at Cape Codd." Julian was only sixteen years old when he became the *Whydah*'s pilot.

Bellamy and his men were fortunate also to have a skilled and experienced physician on board. A doctor on a pirate ship had to be a medical jack-of-all-trades. Pirates fought often, both with their victims and among themselves. A pirate physician, working in an age before anesthesia, antiseptics, and antibiotics, had to be able to quickly amputate a limb and then cauterize the wound with a red-hot ax head (imagine how the patient felt!). He had to treat a host of diseases that pirates often contracted, including scurvy and malaria. The *Whydah*'s doctor, James Ferguson, had worked with Sam Bellamy since 1716, when he joined the crew of the *Marianne* as its doctor. Like so many others, Ferguson's hatred of authority had driven him to become a pirate. He had gone on the account after taking part in an unsuccessful rebellion against England's King George I. Although the record is not clear, Ferguson may have turned to piracy to escape punishment for having participated in the failed revolt.

Another specialist on the *Whydah* was John Brown, in charge of the enormous number of ropes, called lines, on the vessel. Like Dr. Ferguson, Brown had been with Bellamy since the *Marianne* had been his flagship. The unwilling pirate Tom Davis, the carpenter who was forced aboard the *Whydah*, was responsible for repairing damage done to the ship in battle and for maintaining the masts and yardarms.

The most popular of all the specialists on almost every pirate ship, including the *Whydah*, were the members of the vessel's orchestra. Made up of trumpeters, pipers, drummers, fiddlers, harpists, and flutists, the orchestra played for the pirates' enjoyment during their meals and in the evening. They performed a combat role as well. During a battle or while the ship's boarding party was invading a prize vessel, they played loud, aggressive-sounding music to intimidate the enemy and urge on their fellow pirates.

Perhaps more than any other place in the world at that time, a pirate ship functioned as a democracy. As underwater explorer Barry Clifford, who has played a premier role in the twentieth-century chapter of the *Whydah*'s saga, has explained, "It's the story of people who were outlaws but practiced a democracy where former slaves could be elected captains and officers and crew members were treated equally."

Everything of any significance that took place on the *Whydah* was decided by a vote of the crew. The captain was elected and could be removed by another vote at any point except during battle. At that time, the captain's word was law, and anyone who defied him could immediately be put to death by the quartermaster.

Nowhere was the spirit of democracy more in evidence than in the distribution of booty. Racial or ethnic differences among the pirates did not affect the division of the plunder; everything was shared equally. Among the *Whydah*'s crew were African Americans, Africans, Native Americans, Europeans, white Americans, and people of mixed backgrounds, and all of them received the same share of the loot.

This spirit of democracy and equality extended to where those aboard the *Whydah* slept. The only person with his own quarters was Captain Bellamy. But he was expected to share the cabin and even his food and drink with the crew. Typically, the pirates slept in hammocks—but only if there were enough hammocks for everyone. If there were not, everybody slept on the deck.

For men who could be incredibly cruel and violent, pirates went well out of their way to take care of their own. Men on the *Whydah* and other pirate ships who lost eyes or limbs in battle were allowed to remain on the ship for as long as they wished. As one historian has noted, "Many a peg leg clomped over the pirates' decks, earning a half share of plunder as a cook, no matter how little he knew of the culinary arts." The pirates even had early forms of workers' compensation and life insurance. A man who lost a leg on the job received five hundred Spanish pieces of eight. Someone who lost an eye received one hundred. And if a pirate was killed, his family was paid to help compensate for his loss.

Many of the men who chose piracy regarded themselves as

true Robin Hoods, robbing from the rich to give to the poor, and standing in open defiance of all those in authority. Unless they were privateers, acting in the employ of a government, what they were doing was illegal, and they knew that if they were caught, they would end their days swinging from a rope. But it was a life that most chose happily. "In an honest [occupation]," declared pirate Captain Bartholomew Roberts, "there is thin rations, low wages and hard labor; in [piracy, there is] plenty . . . pleasure and ease, liberty and power. . . . A merry life and a short one shall be my motto."

CHAPTER FIVE

The Whydah Rules the Waves

THE MORE HE SAILED IT, the more Bellamy loved the *Whydah.* The pirate Alonzo Batilla had called it the fastest ship in the West Indies. Bellamy agreed. And it was not only fast; it was also the most maneuverable ship he had ever handled.

According to Bellamy's log, in February 1717 the *Whydah,* accompanied only by the *Marianne,* began its life as a pirate ship by steering "away for the Capes of Virginia, being 180 men in company." They soon reached busy shipping lanes and began capturing and looting one prize ship after another. Then, almost without warning, their luck ran out. For four days and three nights, they were forced to battle one of the most violent storms Bellamy had ever encountered. In his book *A General History of the Pyrates,* Daniel Defoe, the author of the fictional classic *Robinson Crusoe,* provided a description of the historic storm. Put into modern English, Defoe's account reads: "The storm increased at twilight with the heavens covered with sheets of lightning. The terrible sound of the roaring winds could only be equaled by the continual clap of thunder, loud enough to frighten the Supreme Being who commands the sea and the winds. . . .

"The men of the *Whydah* and the *Marianne* shouted curses and oaths at the wind and the lightning. Bellamy lamented that the heaving decks would not allow him to fire off his cannons in response to the deafening thunder.

"In the meantime, the wind, amazingly blowing from every direction, increased, and soon the *Whydah*'s mainmast broke in half, and crew members were forced to cut it away. The waves pried two men from the wheel and would have washed them overboard had it not been for the netting that ran along the sides of the ship."

After four days of never knowing whether the next moment would be their last, the pirates felt the storm break almost as abruptly as it had started. But the tempest had left its mark. The decks of both ships were more than ankle-deep in water, and for the better part of a week, the pumps had to be manned day and night. Temporary masts had to be fashioned and raised to replace those lost in the storm, particularly on the *Whydah*. They were called jury masts, and their use gave rise to the term jury-rigged, an expression used today to indicate building something in a makeshift way. And on both vessels, carpenter Tom Davis and his assistants worked feverishly to plug the many leaks caused by the battering waves.

But the pirates had survived, and miraculously, none of their booty had been lost or damaged. The tensions of the past four days were over. Even though there was still much to do, it was time to celebrate. As was common on pirate ships, the crew decided to put on a skit. Several of the pirates suggested they act out one of the crew's favorite short plays, *The Royal Pyrate,* a drama about Alexander the Great. At the height of the skit, with the audience totally caught up in the drama, the pirate playing the role of Alexander captured the pirate playing the hero and ordered that he be hanged. At this point, one of the *Whydah*'s gunners, so immersed in what was going on that he forgot it was only play-acting, mounted the stage and rushed to the pirate's defense. He grabbed a hand grenade, lit its fuse, and threw it at the actors. At the same time, other members of the audience, also engrossed in the drama, grabbed their cutlasses and charged the performers.

Before Bellamy could put a halt to the chaos, the pirate playing Alexander had lost an arm, the pirate whom Alexander had captured had suffered a broken leg from the burst of the grenade, and the pirate who had severed Alexander's limb lay dead on the makeshift stage. When order was restored, both the gunner who had first attacked Alexander and all those who had rushed the stage were clapped into irons for a day. And, brandishing his own sword, Bellamy declared that *The Royal Pyrate* would never again be performed on the *Whydah*.

Once all of the repairs were made, the *Whydah* sailed on. The weather was still not good, and as a dense fog settled in, Bellamy lost sight of Williams and the *Marianne*. The two captains had agreed to spend the next ten days or so seeking prize ships off the Virginia coast, and when the fog finally lifted, Bellamy found himself in the middle of one of the busiest shipping lanes in the Americas. Fortunately, there were no naval vessels on the prowl for pirate ships in the area, and at eight o'clock on the morning of April 17, 1717, the *Whydah*'s lookout spotted the merchant ship *Agnes*, bound from Barbados to Virginia. According to its log, the *Agnes* was laden "with Rum, Sugar and Molasses & Sundry European Goods." After Bellamy and his crew overtook the merchant vessel, forced it to surrender, and boarded it, "the greatest part of the Cargo was plundered by the Pyrates, [and] carry'd on board their Ship."

For the *Whydah*, taking the *Agnes* was just the beginning of a remarkable day. In the next several hours, Bellamy and his crew captured and plundered three more merchant ships—the *Leith*, the *Endeavor*, and the *Ann*. Eight members of the *Leith* voluntarily joined Bellamy's crew. The *Agnes* had taken damage and was

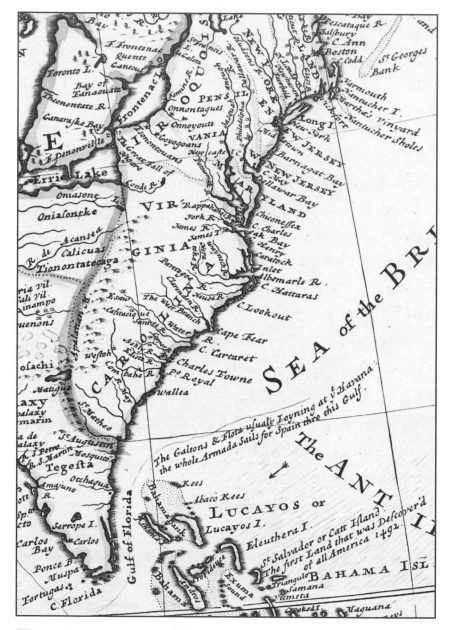

This map shows Sam Bellamy's voyage from the Caribbean to Cape Cod. It also indicates the area off the coast of the colony of Virginia where the Whydah *battled a four-day storm.*

leaking so badly that, according to the final entries in that ship's log, Bellamy transferred its crew to the *Leith* and the *Endeavor* before sending carpenter Tom Davis and his assistants aboard the *Agnes,* where they "cut away the Masts and bored a hole in the bottom of the Vessel, and so destroyed her."

Bellamy then made the *Ann*'s captain and his crew join the *Agnes*'s aboard the *Leith* and the *Endeavor* and allowed them to sail away. But Bellamy had decided to make the *Ann* part of his growing pirate fleet. Putting his quartermaster, Richard Noland, in charge of that vessel, he transferred eighteen of his crew to join those members of the *Ann*'s crew who had decided to become pirates.

When all the transferring of cargo and men was finally completed, the *Whydah* sailed on, and within a few days, the *Marianne* was spotted. During a brief reunion, Bellamy and Williams decided to head for the waters off Rhode Island, which were bound to be filled with cargo-carrying ships at this time of year. They were just nearing Block Island, off the Rhode Island coast, when the *Marianne*'s lookout spied a merchant vessel. It surrendered quickly. On discovering that it was out of Boston, Williams had one of his men row its captain, a man known only as Captain Beer, over to the *Whydah.*

The cargo from Beer's ship was split between the *Whydah* and

A Pirate Attack

WHEN IT CAME TO ATTACKING an enemy ship,
pirates wanted to get as close to their target as possible. The reason was
simple. Their goal was to rob whatever treasure or goods the vessel under
attack was carrying or to capture both the cargo and the vessel itself.
Firing their heavy cannons at their prey risked sinking it, which defeated
the pirates' purposes. Thus, when there wasn't a quick surrender, almost
all pirate attacks were conducted through fierce hand-to-hand combat on
the deck of the targeted ship.

Members of a pirate crew took turns serving as the ship's lookout.
Once they spotted a potential target, great care was taken to make sure
that it was unlikely to overcome them and would yield a great reward.
Spyglasses were used to determine what kind of ship it was, what national
flag it was flying, what kind of cargo it appeared to be carrying, where
it might have been, where it could be headed, and how heavily armed it
was apt to be. Since some lightly armed merchant vessels had fake gun
ports painted on their sides to deceive pirates, it was not always easy to
determine how much of a fight a targeted ship might put up. It was not

unusual for a pirate ship to follow potential prey for hours or even days before deciding whether or not to attack.

As was the pirate way, once the pirates had gathered all the information they could through observation, the decision to attack or withdraw was made by a vote of the entire crew. If, as was almost always the case, the decision was to attack, the pirates went out of their way to terrify their target. They hoisted their Jolly Roger. The musicians produced loud, horrendous noises, and the crew began to "vapor," as they called their practice of dancing around madly, chanting and shouting war cries while waving their muskets, rifles, and cutlasses. If they spotted the vessel's captain, they targeted him for special verbal abuse. "You dog! . . . You speckled-shirted dog!" pirate Captain John Russel shouted at Captain George Roberts of the merchant ship *Dolphin*. "I will drub you, you dog," continued Russel, "within an inch of your life — and that inch too!"

If the prize ship still refused to surrender, the pirates attacked, following a well-established procedure. First, they brought their ship as close to the prize vessel as possible. Next, some crew members lobbed grenades onto the deck of the prize. Some were exploding grenades, designed to cause panic and confusion by setting fires as they landed, and others were smoke grenades, filled with compounds that produced potentially deadly fumes.

While the grenades were flying, other crew members hurled long lines with grappling irons toward the prize vessel. As soon as the sharp points of the grappling irons buried themselves in the prize's deck, pirates pulled on the lines, bringing both ships closer. A third group of pirates, heavily armed and made up of the toughest and boldest men, prepared to board the other vessel. Once aboard, they made quick work of taking control of their prize.

It was a rare occasion when a merchant ship or other vessel dared to challenge a pirate ship. And even though there was competition between pirate captains for booty, and although there were pirate captains who simply did not like each other, it was almost unheard of for one pirate vessel to ignore their time-honored code and attack another.

the *Marianne.* Bellamy and Williams wanted to give Beer back his ship once the captured goods had been transferred, but first they had to put the question to a vote of the crew. From the moment Beer came aboard the *Whydah,* many of the pirates were put off by the arrogance of this man who was, in fact, their prisoner. Almost every man voted to sink his ship. It was up to Bellamy to give Beer the bad news.

Explaining that under the pirates' Articles, he could not overturn a vote of his crew, Bellamy told Beer, "I'm sorry they won't let you have your [ship] again, for I scorn to do anyone mischief when it is not for my advantage. . . . We must sink her." An angry Captain Beer was taken aback. He could not fathom how the captain of a ship could be overruled by his crew. "Surely you and Captain Williams command your crew, and not the other way around?" he exclaimed. "Or perhaps you are no captain at all, but merely a thief obeying your fellow thieves."

Beer's words touched a nerve in Bellamy. Questioning a pirate's right to challenge authority went against everything Bellamy and every pirate he admired stood for. Grabbing Beer by the collar, Bellamy shouted, "Damn you, you are a sneaking puppy—and so are all those who submit to be governed by laws which rich men have made for their own security, for the cowardly whelps have not the courage to defend what they get by their knavery. . . . Damn them for a pack of crafty rascals, and you, who serve them, for a parcel of hen-hearted numskulls. They vilify us, the scoundrels do, when there is only this difference: they rob the poor under the cover of law, and we plunder the rich under the protection of our own courage. Had you not better [become] one of us, than sneak after . . . those villains for employment?"

It was a remarkable way of Bellamy inviting Beer to join the ranks of the pirates. And for a few moments, Beer seemed to be giving it serious consideration. But he could not bring himself to do it. Looking Bellamy in the eye, he stated, "I cannot break the laws of God and man, as you have. You say you're clever, and courageous, but I swear to you now that you'll die by the force of the sea, by the hands of men, or by the hand of God."

Beer's words were more than a refusal to join the pirates. They were Beer's way of telling Bellamy that he did not have as much power as a pirate captain as he believed he had. For this, the captain of the *Whydah* had a ready answer. "You are a devilish rascal. . . . I am a free prince, and I have as much authority to make war on the whole world as he who has a hundred sail of ships at sea, and an army of one hundred thousand men in the field; and this my conscience tells me."

Having said his piece, Bellamy was done with Captain Beer. He dismissed him and had one of his men row him to Block

Island and leave him there to find his way back to his home in Newport, Rhode Island. Meanwhile, Bellamy was preparing to sail the *Whydah* to Maine to plunder more prizes before putting the ship ashore to have its bottom scraped and cleaned and to make other necessary repairs. Williams had his own plans. His mother, his sister, and his niece lived on Block Island. Williams would remain anchored there for several days while he visited with them. Then he would sail the *Marianne* to a predetermined spot in Maine, where he would rejoin Bellamy and the *Whydah* and they would, he was certain, resume their pattern of pursuing and capturing every cargo-carrying vessel that fell within their sights.

CHAPTER SIX

The Wreck of the Whydah

WILLIAMS HAD NO WAY of knowing that just after he left his partner, Bellamy would make a decision that remains the greatest mystery in the saga of the *Whydah*. At first, Bellamy ordered the men at the *Whydah*'s wheel to skirt Cape Cod and continue northward toward Maine as he and Williams had planned. A few hours later, he abruptly told them to change course and head directly to Cape Cod. For some three hundred years, those intrigued by the story of the *Whydah* have asked themselves why Sam Bellamy changed his plan.

Among the most popular theories is that, having made himself the richest of all the pirates, Bellamy decided to return to Maria Hallett to show her parents how wealthy he had become and to carry her off to a Caribbean island as he had promised her. Those who doubt that there ever was a Maria Hallett believe that it was the extraordinary riches carried by the *Whydah* that suddenly motivated Bellamy to stop looking for prize vessels and head for Cape Cod. With more money in his hold than he or any of his men would ever be able to spend, he had the opportunity to return to a place he loved, sell his enormous cargo, pay his crew members, and let them go off to luxurious retirement.

Whatever his reason for aiming for the Cape, his voyage was interrupted early on April 24, 1717. As he was passing the island of Nantucket, just south of Cape Cod, a crew member spotted a merchant ship off in the distance. Bellamy gave chase, and at 9:30 in the morning, the *Whydah* caught up to its latest prize vessel.

Originally out of Dublin, Ireland, and commanded by a Captain Crumpstey, the *Mary Anne* was a flat-bottomed ship called a pink. Crumpstey briefly entertained thoughts of putting up a fight, even though he had only a small crew, but after seven cutlass-wielding pirates jumped aboard the *Mary Anne* and threatened mayhem, he told them that his ship was theirs.

As the seven pirates took Captain Crumpstey to the *Whydah* to meet with Bellamy, a larger boarding party from the pirate ship rowed toward their prize to begin transferring its cargo to their vessel. Once aboard, they received an enormous and most welcome surprise: the *Mary Anne* was carrying more than seven thousand gallons of Madeira wine. After having plundered more gold and silver and other treasure than they could ever have imagined, the pirates had stumbled upon the greatest loot of all—all the fine wine they could drink.

Given its special cargo, Bellamy decided to add the pink to his flotilla, and the *Whydah,* the *Ann,* and the *Mary Anne,* sailing in tandem, continued toward the coast of Cape Cod. But Bellamy had a serious concern. He had lived in Eastham, and he knew that the waters off the Cape were among the most treacherous in the world. As a thick fog was setting in, he put one of his most experienced sailors in the crow's nest to look for the darker blue water that indicated the deepest spots. He had another pirate take constant soundings to make sure that they would avoid shallow seas.

But then Bellamy had a stroke of luck. In the distance, another merchant vessel was spotted. The *Whydah* gave chase and soon caught up to the prize, the *Fisher,* which had been on its way to Virginia from Boston. According to the *Fisher*'s log, it was "laden with Tobacco, hides and other things." But this time Bellamy was not interested in plunder. What he needed was information. Even though he regarded both his crewman known only as Lambeth and the young John Julian as able pilots, he feared that they were not as familiar with the dangerous Cape Cod waters as they would need to be in the case of a severe storm. Shouting over to the *Fisher*'s captain, Robert Ingols, Bellamy asked if he was acquainted with these waters, and, to Bellamy's relief, Ingols shouted back that he knew the coastline "very well."

Immediately Bellamy ordered Ingols to come aboard the

Whydah and sent four heavily armed pirates across to the *Fisher* to make sure that the vessel followed Bellamy's small flotilla. As night descended, the *Whydah,* the *Ann,* the *Mary Anne,* and the *Fisher,* all with lanterns ablaze at their sterns, made their way along the dangerous coastline, the most treacherous of all from Florida to Maine.

The famous American author Henry David Thoreau, a keen observer of Cape Cod, wrote that so many ships were wrecked off the Cape that "the inhabitants hear the crash of vessels going to pieces as they sit round their hearths." On April 26, 1717, as the weather rapidly deteriorated, Bellamy's fleet continued along the Cape. Around ten o'clock in the evening, the wind began to gust up to eighty miles per hour, and heavy rain squalls pounded the pirate fleet. The seas rose above fifty feet, and huge bolts of lightning streaked across the sky. Bellamy could not know that an Arctic gale from Canada was colliding with a warm front racing northward from the Caribbean. It was what meteorologists call a perfect storm, and one of the worst ever to hit Cape Cod.

As the winds increased and the seas grew as rough as Bellamy had ever seen them, Black Sam turned to Ingols, who had assured him that he knew how to deal with Cape Cod storms. But Ingols had lied. Not only was he unfamiliar with the Cape coastline and its weather, but he now appeared to be on the verge of panic.

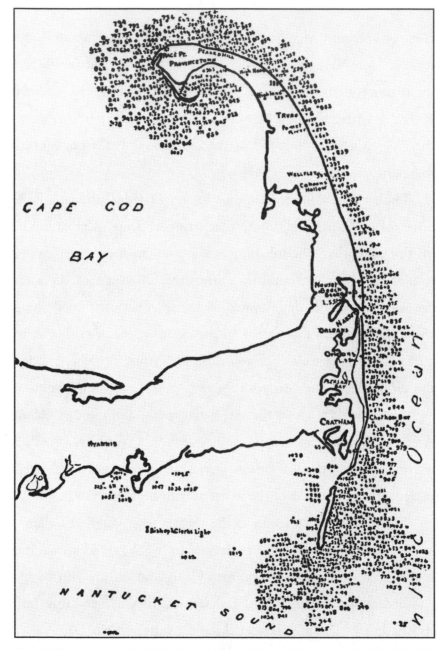

Cape Cod began to earn the dubious honor of being known as "the graveyard of the Atlantic" almost as soon as explorers and settlers from Europe began to appear on its shores. This map, drawn in the early 1900s, shows an amazing number of shipwreck sites up to the year 1903.

Desperate for help, Bellamy shouted over to the *Ann,* which was riding the waves perilously close to the *Whydah.* Although Bellamy had placed his former quartermaster Richard Noland in charge of the *Ann* when he captured it, that vessel's former captain, a man known only as Montgomery, was still on board it as well. From conversations he had had with Montgomery, Bellamy had the impression that, unlike Ingols, Montgomery did know his way around the Cape Cod coast.

Hanging on to the *Whydah'*s rail for dear life, Bellamy kept shouting over the storm for Montgomery. When he appeared, clutching at his own rail, Bellamy made Montgomery a promise: if he guided them to Provincetown Harbor, he would earn back his freedom and his ship.

Montgomery immediately agreed and made his way to the *Ann'*s wheel. But not trusting that Bellamy would keep his word, he had his own plans. Knowing that the *Ann* was much lighter than the larger, treasure-laden *Whydah,* Montgomery told Bellamy to follow him and that he would guide him into Provincetown Harbor. Montgomery actually intended to lead Bellamy to an area of treacherous sandbars over which the lighter *Ann* could safely pass but upon which the heavy *Whydah* would run aground and, in such a devastating storm, be torn apart.

For a time, Bellamy followed Montgomery and the *Ann,* but

it became obvious to him that Montgomery was not heading to safety but straight toward shore. He tried to change course, but the wind was too strong. Next he ordered the crew to drop the vessel's half-ton anchors overboard. Many of the *Whydah*'s crew climbed into the rigging to escape the waves washing over the deck.

Still, the *Whydah* was drawn closer and closer to the treacherous shoreline. As Thomas Davis later remembered, Bellamy stood defiantly on the deck as he had done during the terrible storm off the coast of Virginia a month before, shouting "blasphemies, oaths, and horrid imprecations" to the heavens. Bellamy was again ready to order the crew to fire the ship's cannons skyward in response to the almost deafening ceaseless thunder.

As its captain railed against the sky, the *Whydah* was shaken by an enormous jolt. Just as Montgomery had intended, Bellamy's ship had slammed into a sandbar. The jolt was so severe that it threw sailors from the rigging into the freezing sea. Before anyone on board could react, a gigantic wave slammed into and over the *Whydah,* tearing all of its more than sixty cannons from their mounts. As they careened across the deck, the cannons crushed every unfortunate pirate who stood in their path. Breaking loose, heavy cannonballs and barrels filled with nails crashed through the deck and killed those whom they fell upon below.

It only got worse. Shortly after midnight, the *Whydah*'s

mainmast snapped, and the heavily loaded ship was drawn into shallow water, where it overturned. Then the ultimate catastrophe took place. The *Whydah*'s hull broke apart, and the dead and those who were still living were cast into the pounding surf.

Within minutes, most of the pirates who had been thrown into the sea died from the frigid ocean temperatures. Among the dead was John King, the young boy who had dared threaten his own mother so that he could sail with his hero, Black Sam Bellamy. His hero drowned, too.

Bellamy, who had just become the most successful pirate of his day, was killed by the rarest of storms. Killed by one of the few captains to defy his orders. Killed, according to many, within sight of the house of the sweetheart who may have been the reason he returned to the Cape.

The *Whydah* met its spectacular end on one of the most desolate stretches of coast on thinly settled Cape Cod. Yet by the very next morning, scores of inhabitants were scouring the site of the wreck, hopeful of finding treasure either lying on the shoreline or floating in the sea.

Nothing excited Cape Codders more than a shipwreck. Local newspapers were fond of telling the stories of schoolchildren who, as they sat by their classroom windows, paid far more attention to looking for ships in distress than they did to their lessons.

An Ocean Graveyard

HISTORIANS ESTIMATE that some thirty-five hundred ships have fallen prey to the vicious storms and hidden sandbars in the fifty-mile stretch of Cape Cod coastline between Chatham and Provincetown. More than a thousand of these shipwrecks lie between the towns of Truro and Wellfleet alone, a distance of only five miles.

The first recorded shipwreck off Cape Cod took place in 1626. The *Sparrowhawk*, bound for the early colony of Jamestown, Virginia, ran aground in a storm after having sailed three thousand miles from England. The twenty-five people aboard managed to get safely to shore, and the ship was repaired. But before it could resume its journey, it was struck by another storm and wasn't seen again for more than two hundred years. In 1863, yet another great storm partially uncovered the *Sparrowhawk*, allowing much of its hull and other parts of the ship to be salvaged, and providing naval historians valuable information about the hull design and construction of the earliest ships used to settle the New World.

Visitors to the Boston Common view the reconstructed hull of the Sparrowhawk, *as was pictured in* Frank Leslie's Illustrated, *October 21, 1869.*

In the late 1700s and early 1800s, there was an average of two shipwrecks a month off the Cape Cod coast, particularly in winter. When a storm hit, it was almost expected that the alarm "Ship ashore! All hands perishing!" would be heard on land. Citizens would rush to the beach, but almost always the waves were too high for them to even attempt a rescue.

It was not until 1872 that things began to change. In that year, the U.S. government created the first truly efficient coastal lifesaving service. Lifesaving stations built every five miles along the Cape Cod coast were each manned by six or seven surfmen and a station keeper, who kept

Members of the United States Life-Saving Service head out to sea in an attempt to rescue passengers from a wrecked ship off Cape Cod.

a constant lookout for ships in distress. At night, men from the stations patrolled the beach, ready to summon aid for any vessel in trouble.

Whenever a ship in distress was sighted, one of the members of the lifesaving crew fired off a red flare, letting those on the stricken ship know that help was on the way. Then, if the sea permitted it, the lifesaving crew launched their special oversize surfboats and raced to the aid of the shipwrecked mariners. If the sea was too rough to allow surfboats to be launched, the lifesaving team stayed on the beach and, using a small cannon called a Lyle gun, fired a double line with a pulley to the stricken ship. Then they pulled the crew safely to shore, one by one, in a basket-like device called a breeches buoy.

Thanks to the introduction of the lifesaving service and the building of the Cape Cod Canal, which allows ships to avoid many of the Cape's most dangerous waters, the rate of shipwrecks has been greatly reduced. But the devastating storms and hidden sandbars still remain. And despite the extraordinary advancements in ship construction and navigational technology, every captain worth his or her salt knows that the waters that form the vast graveyard of the *Whydah* and so many other ships must be treated with caution and respect.

Whenever they spied one, the newspapers reported, they bolted from the classroom, accompanied not only by their classmates but by their teachers as well.

To those who lived on Cape Cod, shipwrecks were so important that many adopted the old English prayer "We pray Thee, O Lord, not that wrecks should happen, but that if any shall happen, Thou wilt guide them onto our shores for the benefit of the inhabitants."

The benefits that were provided to the nearby residents were sometimes so great that many Cape Codders were unwilling to leave shipwrecks to chance. The citizens of one Cape town protested vehemently against building a lighthouse on the grounds that it would undoubtedly reduce the number of shipwrecks. Even more unprincipled citizens deliberately caused ships to run aground by sending false signals to them. By waving a lantern from a beach, saboteurs could convince a ship's captain to head their way. Believing that the light indicated the direction where he could safely navigate the dangerous coastal waters, the captain would instead run his ship aground. Because the strategy worked only on moonless nights, when the coastline could not be seen, those who caused wrecks this way were given the name "mooncussers."

While any shipwreck would set Cape Codders racing to the disaster, one can only imagine the excitement, even the frenzy, that was caused when word spread that a pirate ship had been destroyed on the outer beach between Eastham and Wellfleet. This was not only a chance to plunder a wrecked ship's wood, canvas, foodstuffs, or other common items that it might have aboard, but a once-in-a-lifetime opportunity to perhaps lay one's hands on gold or silver or other unimaginable riches. Many Cape Codders were unable to resist such a temptation.

CHAPTER SEVEN

The Survivors

OF THE 146 MEN aboard the *Whydah*, only two survived the disaster. Somehow Thomas Davis and young John Julian were able to swim ashore and climb the steep sand dunes. They then made their way to the nearby house of farmer Samuel Harding, who, with his wife, stood wide-eyed as Davis told him what had happened to the *Whydah* and its crew.

Harding could not help but feel sorry for Davis's crewmates. But in the sailors' bad fortune, he saw opportunity. Harding, like the majority of Cape farmers, was barely making a living. There had to be goods in the *Whydah* wreckage that he could use. The next morning, he hitched up his wagon and took Davis and Julian down to the shore. They brought back several loads of goods that he hid in his barn. Harding's good luck was bad for Davis and Julian. A number of locals saw them aiding the farmer and guessed that the strangers were from the wreck. Carrying out what they saw as their civic duty, the townspeople informed the local authorities, who arrested Davis and Julian and placed them in jail.

While only two men from the *Whydah* came out of the storm alive, seven of the some sixty pirates and original crew aboard the *Mary Anne* survived. When the *Whydah,* the *Mary Anne,* the *Ann,* and the *Fisher* had been making their way up the coast, the *Mary Anne* had been in the lead. Up to that point, the seven men whom Bellamy had transferred onto the *Mary Anne* from the *Whydah* had considered themselves the luckiest pirates alive, being placed on a ship filled with cases of fine wine. But the *Mary Anne* developed a serious leak and fell to the rear. As they manned the pumps nonstop, the crew "damn'd the Vessel and wished they had never seen her."

And then things got even worse. With a great shudder and roar, the *Mary Anne* smashed into a sandbar. Only the quick thinking of the pirate Thomas Baker, who immediately cut down two of the vessel's masts, prevented it from meeting the same fate as the *Whydah*. Its crew knew they had to flee the area before the authorities, always eager to get their hands on pirates, arrived. As they were making their plans to escape, a canoe pulled up to the stricken ship. Aboard it were two men, John Cole and William Smith, who had spotted the wreck and offered to take the crew back to the mainland. But as they rowed toward shore, Cole and Smith overheard the men they had rescued making plans to find their way to a pirate haven in Rhode Island, where they felt they would be sheltered. As soon as they were alone, Cole and Smith reported their plans to the Eastham sheriff. All seven were arrested and placed in jail in the nearby town of Barnstable.

The pirates aboard the *Ann* and the *Fisher* fared much better. As the devious Captain Montgomery had planned, the *Ann* had led the unsuspecting *Whydah* toward the sandbars and then, under the cover of darkness and the storm, had turned back out to sea, where it anchored next to the *Fisher* to ride out the storm. The *Fisher*, however, began leaking badly, and those aboard it transferred its loot to the *Ann* and opened all the hatches on the *Fisher*. Tons of water poured in, and the *Fisher* was sent to a watery grave. With that accomplished, the *Ann*, captained by the *Whydah*'s former quartermaster Richard Noland, set sail for Maine, hoping to meet up with Bellamy, the *Whydah*, and the *Marianne*. When the *Whydah* failed to appear, Noland and the men of the *Ann* began a long series of successful raids on ships all the way from Maine to the Bahamas.

All of which adds more mystery to the *Whydah* saga. Montgomery's actions in leading the *Whydah* to its tragic end are well documented. So too is the fact that the *Ann*, captained by Richard Noland, captured a considerable amount of loot from ships sailing in the waters between Maine and the Bahamas in the months following the *Whydah*'s sinking. But what about Captain

Montgomery? Was he still aboard the *Ann* when these raids were staged? Was he a willing participant or was he a prisoner of Noland and his pirates? We simply don't know.

What we do know is that Richard Noland had a unique ending to his career in piracy. In 1718, he abruptly accepted King George I's offer of a pardon to any pirate. Noland, according to Daniel Defoe, lived out the rest of his life as a model citizen and died peacefully, something extremely rare for someone who had spent most of his life on the account.

Paulsgrave Williams also ended his days in a much different fashion from most pirates. After spending time with his mother, sister, and niece on Block Island, Williams sailed to the spot in Maine where he and Bellamy had agreed to meet. Two weeks after he arrived at the meeting site, word reached Williams of the wreck of the *Whydah*.

Sick at heart, Williams sailed to the pirate haven at New Providence, in the Bahamas. He next appears in the historical record in 1720, serving as an officer aboard a pirate ship commanded by his old friend Olivier LeBous. Three years later, at the age of forty-five, Williams retired from piracy, settled down with a new wife, and began a family. The man who had provided the funds that enabled Sam Bellamy to become his era's most successful pirate, the man who had accompanied Bellamy on all of his greatest adventures, would, unlike Bellamy, live a long life and die a peaceful death.

For the nine imprisoned pirates, the seven months they spent awaiting trial in the Boston jail to which they had all been transferred was the worst period of their lives. In the beginning, not a single day went by without their hoping that a group of their fellow pirates, particularly Paulsgrave Williams and his men, would storm the prison and rescue them. But as days turned into weeks and weeks turned into months, even the most optimistic of them lost all hope of rescue. The one thing the prisoners learned they could count on was an almost daily visit from one of the most influential religious leaders in the colonies, the Puritan minister Cotton Mather. A scientist and historian as well as a minister, at fifteen he had become the youngest man ever to graduate from Harvard College, and he went on to publish 382 books in his lifetime. Mather took a particular interest in the imprisoned pirates. His constant visits to the jail were made for a single purpose: to get them to confess to their crimes, something they steadfastly refused to do.

Finally, on October 18, 1717, seven prisoners were brought to trial. After six months in a dark prison cell, the bright glare of the Boston courtroom practically blinded them. Their long diet of bread and water had left them looking like skeletons. They were still wearing the clothes they had worn on the night they were arrested.

Cotton Mather was not only one of the most influential men in the American colonies, but he was also involved in more endeavors than probably any other person of his time. He was a champion of education for African Americans, worked toward establishing libraries for working people, and helped establish societies to carry out other types of charitable work.

As they stood nervously waiting for their trial to begin, the thirteen men who would decide their fate filed slowly into the courtroom and took their places at a long table in front of the accused. Included among them were some of the highest-ranking officials of the royal province of Massachusetts Bay, including Samuel Shute, the governor and commander in chief of the province; William Dummer, lieutenant governor of the province; and three members of the King's Council for the province.

Before the largest crowd ever to have been packed into the huge courtroom, the charges against the accused were read. "So it is," proclaimed one of the court officials, "that . . . Simon Van Vorst, John Brown, Thomas South, Thomas Baker, Hendrick Quintor, Peter Cornelius Hoof, and John Shuan, To the High displeasure of Almighty God, in open Violation of the Rights of Nations and Mankind, and in Contempt and Defyance of His Majesty's good and wholesome Laws aforesaid, Willfully, Wickedly, and Feloniously . . . Perpetrated and Committed on the high Sea sundry Acts of Piracy and Robbery."

The court official also made clear just what the penalty would be if any or all of the pirates were found guilty of the crimes of which they were accused. "That such Persons," he declared, "as shall be . . . found Guilty of Piracy, Robbery & Felony committed in, or upon the Sea or in any Haven, River, Creek or Place where the Admiral or Admirals have Power, Authority or Jurisdiction, by their own Confessions, or their Refusing to Plead, or upon the Oath of Witnesses . . . shall be Executed and put to Death."

With the charges read and the penalty for these crimes made clear, each of the accused was asked to state how he pleaded. After each proclaimed himself to be not guilty, it was time for the king's Advocate, known only as Mr. Smith, to make his case. He began by reminding the court of what a singularly horrendous crime piracy was. Piracy, Smith declared, involved "Treason, Oppression, Murder, Assassination, Robbery and Theft." It was, Smith stated, carried out "in remote and Solitary Places, where the weak and Defenceless can expect no Assistance nor Relief." That stated, Smith then informed the court that he would be introducing a number of witnesses whose testimony would prove that "the Prisoners are all and each of them Guilty."

Smith's first witness was Thomas Fitzgerald, who had been a mate aboard the wine-carrying *Mary Anne*. He testified that Bellamy and his men "all Armed with Mosquets, Pistols and Cutlasses" had "forcibly taken Command" of that ship. Fitzgerald then described how the *Whydah*'s pirates plundered the large cargo of wine and stole "some Cloaths which belonged to the Ship's Company." He made specific mention of how pirate Simon Van Vorst had threatened to break the cook's neck "if he would not find Liquor" for the marauding pirates.

More Than a Trial

THE TRIAL of the *Whydah* pirates drew huge interest throughout the American colonies, but particularly in Boston, where the proceedings took place. It was about much more than the guilt or innocence of the men who stood before the court. In becoming pirates, the men of the *Whydah*, like almost all of their counterparts, declared themselves to be their own men, above all authority. The British government regarded the trials and executions of any pirates they could catch as important opportunities to demonstrate to the public and all other pirates that true authority lay with the king, the government, and the Church.

Sam Bellamy and his men terrorized the shipping lanes in an era that placed great value on rituals. And in its determination to demonstrate its authority, the British government followed three procedures in dealing with the pirates they apprehended: the trial itself, sermons directed at the accused pirates, and the execution of all pirates convicted of their crimes.

The purpose of the trial was to reveal that pirates were subhuman creatures and the enemies of mankind. It was designed to be great theater. Court officials explained the nature of the pirates' crimes and argued that their crimes exceeded all other transgressions and that the pirates needed not only to be convicted, but also to receive the harshest punishment possible. The Puritan Church regarded pirates as the worst of all sinners and ensured that, as pirate historian Philip Gosse has written, constant sermons were directed at the convicted, so that "almost every hour between the passing of the sentence and the carrying out of the execution was devoted to the spiritual salvation of the condemned."

As the author Andrew Harken Hall has observed, "The struggle for authority between pirates and the government ended in the hanging of the pirate and then the public display of his corpse." This final ritual was designed to hammer home the message that there were brutal consequences to being a pirate. "Thus we see what a disastrous Fate, ever attends the Wicked," wrote Daniel Defoe in his *General History of the Pyrates*. "'Tis to be hoped that the Examples of these Deaths . . . warn others from the same Shipwreck and Ruin for the Future."

Though many pirates met this fate, their legends survived long after them, and the romantic way in which they were regarded by so many still lives with us today.

One of the next to testify was Thomas Checkley, who had been a sailor aboard the merchant ship *Tanner*, which had been captured by the *Whydah* in March 1717. Checkley testified that, despite anything the accused might say about being forced to become pirates, he had seen firsthand that Captain Bellamy and his men "forced no Body to go with them" and "would take no Body against their Wills." As an example, Checkley described how his shipmate John Shuan had "declared himself to be now a Pirate" and "went up and unriggd the Main top-mast by order of the [*Whydah*] pyrates."

There then followed other individuals, all of whom swore that they had been eyewitness to the fact that each of the accused was a member of the *Whydah*'s crew and, as such, had performed the types of crimes with which they were charged. When these witnesses completed their testimony, the pirates were told to step forward and asked "what they had to say for themselves."

Before the trial had begun, the accused had decided that their only chance of saving themselves was to claim that they were not really pirates at all but had been forced, on pain of death, by Sam Bellamy to serve aboard his ships. Among the pirates who testified was Thomas Baker, who stated that after he had been captured and (according to him) forced to become a pirate, "he attempted to make his escape at Spanish Town" when the *Whydah* docked at what was then the capital of Jamaica. According to Baker's testimony, "the Governour of that Place seemed to favour his design, till Capt. Bellamy and his Company sent the Governour word that they would burn & destroy the Town" if the governor helped Baker escape.

Thomas South swore that, as a member of a crew of a ship that had sailed from Bristol, England, he was captured by Bellamy and "threatened to be put upon a desolate Island, where there was nothing to support him" unless he became a member of the *Whydah*'s pirate crew. Peter Cornelius Hoof also testified that he had been taken aboard the *Whydah* against his wishes and told by its crew that "they would kill him unless he would joyn with them in their Unlawful Designs." Hendrick Quintor also swore that he had been captured by Bellamy, who, after agreeing to release Quintor when they reached the coast of Venezuela, changed his mind, causing Quintor to be "unavoidably forced to Continue among the Pyrates."

After others of the accused had offered similar testimony, His Majesty's Advocate Smith responded to the pirates' claims. And, from his first remarks, it was clear that he had absolutely no sympathy for them. "Their pretence of being forced out of the respective Ships and Vessels they belonged to, by Bellamy . . . if it [is] true, can never excuse their Guilt," he declared, "since no case of Necessity can justify a direct violation of . . . Law, and give one the liberty of Sinning." Besides, continued Smith, "That [the accused] acted freely and by their own choice is most plain and obvious."

When Smith concluded his remarks, the court was adjourned in order to give the judges time to decide upon a verdict. In late October 1717, the proceedings were reconvened, and Governor Shute, in his role as president of the court, read its verdict. "The Court," declared Shute, "having duly considered the Indictment & the Proofs of the several articles contained therein, together with your Defences, Have found you Simon Van Vorst, John Brown, Thomas Baker, Hendrick Quintor, Peter Cornelius Hoof and John Shuan, Guilty, of the Crimes of Piracy, Robbery and Felony, as is set forth in the Indictment, And do therefore Adjudge and Decree, That you Simon Van Vorst, John Brown, Thomas Baker, Hendrick Quintor, Peter Cornelius Hoof, and John Shuan, shall go hence to the Place from whence you came, and from thence you shall be carried to the Place of Execution, and there you and each of you, shall be hanged up by the Neck until you & each of you are Dead; And the Lord have Mercy on your Souls."

Then Governor Shute, in an announcement that probably shocked the large courtroom crowd, declared that the judges had concluded that Thomas South had, in fact, been forcibly taken from his ship and "compelled utterly against his Will to joyn with the Pirates." The Court, Shute announced, had found him not guilty.

South would not be the only pirate to escape the hangman's noose. After receiving testimonials on his behalf, the judges held a separate trial for Thomas Davis. Written statements from the captain and crew members of the merchant ship *St. Michael* left no doubt that Davis, like Thomas South, had been forced into piracy by Sam Bellamy. Like South, Thomas Davis was found not guilty.

The *Whydah*'s young Miskito Indian pilot, John Julian, also escaped the hangman. In fact, he never appeared in court. Although the records are not totally clear, it appears that he was taken out of jail and sold into slavery before his fellow pirates were tried. Some records state that the man who bought Julian was John Quincy, the great-grandfather of U.S. president John Quincy Adams. Other records indicate that Julian was eventually sold to another man and that he made several attempts to escape. These records indicate that on one of these attempts, Julian killed a bounty hunter who was trying to catch him and that he was executed in 1733.

November 15, 1717, was the date set for, as one Boston newspaper expressed it, "the Execution of these Miserables." Accompanied by dozens of sheriffs and other officials, the condemned pirates were led out of the jail and marched through the streets of Boston to the harbor and Scarlett's Wharf. At the front of the procession was the admiralty marshal, holding above his

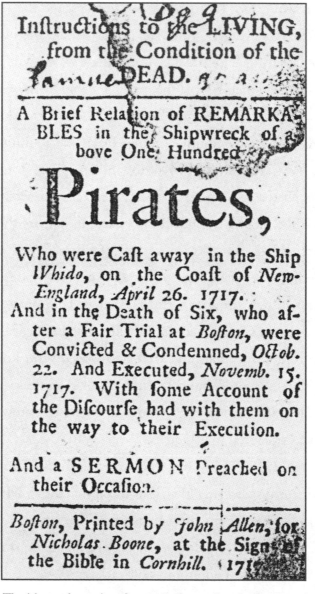

Instructions to the LIVING,
from the Condition of the
DEAD.

A Brief Relation of REMARKA-
BLES in the Shipwreck of a-
bove One Hundred

Pirates,

Who were Caſt away in the Ship
Whido, on the Coaſt of *New-
England*, *April* 26. 1717.
And in the Death of Six, who after a Fair Trial at *Boſton*, were
Convicted & Condemned, *Octob.*
22. And Executed, *Novemb.* 15.
1717. With ſome Account of
the Diſcourſe had with them on
the way to their Execution.

And a SERMON Preached on
their Occaſion.

Boſton, Printed by *John Allen*, for
Nicholas Boone, at the Sign of
the Bible in *Cornhill*. 171

*The title page from a sixty-four-page volume written by Cotton
Mather that included the sermon he preached to the condemned
Whydah pirates and his remarks to them on their way to be executed.*

head what was called the silver oar, the symbol of the Admiralty Court's jurisdiction over crimes that took place at sea.

It was a long, slow march, made longer by the fact that the streets leading to the wharf were packed to overflowing with spectators who had been lining up since early morning to witness the solemn procession as it passed by. Walking every step of the way with the prisoners was Cotton Mather, once again ceaselessly urging the pirates to confess their crimes. Even when they reached the wharf and were rowed across Boston Harbor to the hanging place in Charlestown, Mather pleaded with the pirates to confess.

Finally, standing before the gallows, each of the pirates, in a final, desperate attempt to save their lives, did confess. It did them no good. As each man was hanged, the enormous crowd that had gathered to watch the spectacle let out a mighty roar. Staring at the six bodies swaying in the wind, Cotton Mather exclaimed, "Behold, the End of Piracy." He was not completely correct, but he was close.

Long after everyone had left the hanging place, the bodies kept swaying in the wind. And they kept on swaying—for days, for weeks, for months, and remarkably, for years, until they finally decayed and were gone. The sight was a gruesome warning to anyone who would even consider becoming a pirate.

CHAPTER EIGHT

The Adventures of Cyprian Southack

EVEN AS Thomas Davis and John Julian were helping farmer Samuel Harding scavenge through the remains of the ship that had been their home, news of the wreck was spreading. Within a day, it reached Boston, where Governor Samuel Shute received a handwritten note from a Cape official, stating, "The Pyrate Ship commanded by Capt. Samuel Bellamy, was Shipwreckt [on the shore of Eastham] whereof about 130 Men were drown'd and none saved except two Men, an English Man and an Indian that were cast on Shore. . . . A great many Men have been taken up Dead near the Place where the Ship was cast away."

Shute immediately thought of another Province of Massachusetts Bay governor, Sir William Phips, who, prior to becoming governor, had made himself famous by recovering a fortune from a Spanish treasure ship that had sunk in Florida waters and had made himself rich from the percentage of the gold and silver he received as a result of his accomplishment. Under British

*As well as being a treasure hunter and governor, William Phips was a ship's carpenter,
a ship's captain, and a major general.*

law, Shute, as a government official, would not be able to personally keep anything recovered from the wreck, but he knew he would be certain to gain enormous favor from the king. He faced a major challenge in acting quickly enough to prevent Cape Cod farmers and other locals from carrying off all the treasure. Fifty-five-year-old Cyprian Southack, an acclaimed naval commander and mapmaker, was just the man for the job.

At ten o'clock on the morning of May 1, 1717, Southack, along with several militiamen assigned to him, boarded the British sloop *Nathaniel* and headed to Cape Cod and the site of the *Whydah* wreck. His orders were clear. He was to attempt to recover and bring back to Boston "Money, Bullion, Treasure, Goods and Merchandizes taken out of the said Ship." He was also to take into custody any pirates who might be hiding out after surviving the wreck.

What should have been a quick, uneventful sea journey from Boston to Cape Cod did not go well. Shortly after Southack sailed out of Boston Harbor, pirates stole more than eighty pounds of his supplies. He was further delayed by headwinds that battered his small vessel. Finally on May 2, 1717, he reached Cape Cod Harbor (now called Provincetown Harbor), where he sent two of his men ahead to obtain horses and ride to the wreck site so that they could secure the beach as soon as possible. The men reached the site at seven that evening, but it had been six days since the

Whydah had gone down. By this time, anything from the ship that had lain strewn along the beach had been carted off and hidden in local barns, cellars, and attics.

Meanwhile, Southack and the other eight men of his party, eager to join their two companions at the wreck site, waited in Provincetown. Relying on an old map that showed a natural canal that crossed Cape Cod and ended at Nauset Harbor, a few miles from where the *Whydah* had met its fate, Southack and his men obtained a whaleboat, lugged it to the canal, and began to row. The canal had grown shallower since their map was drawn, and it was not long before their boat hit bottom. They proceeded to create poles out of nearby ash trees, place the poles horizontally directly beneath the heavy whaleboat, and, by gripping the ends of the poles, carry the vessel a great distance, until they reached water deep enough to allow them to row again. Finally they arrived at Nauset Harbor, only to encounter more problems. The ocean was churned up with large waves, and it took every ounce of energy that the nine men had left to row the whaleboat through the heavy seas. Fourteen hours after they had left Provincetown, they reached what Southack would later refer to as the "Pirritt Rack" (pirate wreck).

After suffering such an ordeal just to reach the wreck, Southack could not have been more disappointed at what lay before him.

Cyprian Southack

BEFORE HE EVEN ARRIVED on Cape Cod, Cyprian Southack, appointed by Massachusetts colonial governor Samuel Shute to prevent the looting of the *Whydah* wreck, was a man already known for his seamanship and for his mapmaking skills. Born in 1662, Southack followed in the footsteps of his father, a British naval lieutenant. He was only ten years old when he assisted his father in the Battle of Southwold Bay between British and Dutch naval forces off the coast of England in 1672.

In 1685, at the age of twenty-three, Southack was sent by the British Admiralty to the Province of Massachusetts Bay, where, as captain of the armed ship *Province Galley*, he took part in a long series of battles and expeditions against the French for control of North America. As captain of the *Province Galley*, Southack was also charged with guarding the Massachusetts coastline against pirates.

None of these activities represented his true passion. Cyprian Southack's great love was making maps. At that time, maps of the long New England coastline were rare and inaccurate. Southack committed himself to producing maps that became invaluable to mariners sailing the Eastern seaboard, particularly from New England to Nova Scotia. The maps that Southack drew were arguably the most accurate of their time, so much so that for at least half a century after he died they were used to navigate the New England coast.

Southack is known to have produced at least twenty detailed maps of areas along the New England coast. His greatest cartographical contribution was a publication that came to be used almost as a bible by mariners. Called *The New England Coasting Pilot,* it contained eight maps alongside more than one hundred descriptive notes from Southack's voyages up and down the New England coast.

The notes reveal Southack's interest in providing mariners with more than just navigational information. Along with indicating navigational hazards, water depths, and tides and currents, they also mark fishing grounds, places containing timber for masts and shipbuilding, and fish-drying sites. Cyprian Southack was not a modest man, and he was not above naming some of the locations he mapped after himself. For example, in his map of Maine, Monhegan Island is called "Southacks Island or Monhegan," and the present Chedabucto Bay in Nova Scotia was named Southacks Bay. Southack was also not averse to citing his personal accomplishments on the maps. Thus, in indicating the location of the Strait of Canso between Nova Scotia and Cape Breton Island, he added the notation that in 1690 he became the first Englishman to sail through it.

He may have been immodest, but Cyprian Southack was certainly one of the most important mapmakers in colonial America. And one map that he drew after arriving on Cape Cod would become instrumental in the discovery of the ship known as the *Whydah*.

The title page of Cyprian Southack's guide to the waters off of the northeastern United States and southeastern Canada.

THE

NEW ENGLAND

COASTING PILOT

FROM

SANDY POINT of NEW YORK,

UNTO

Cape C A N S O in Nova Scotia,

And Part of *Ifland B R E T O N.*

WITH THE

COURSES and DISTANCES from Place to Place, and TOWNS on the Sea-Board; HARBOURS, BAYS, ISLANDS, ROADS, ROCKS, SANDS: The Setting and Flowing of TIDES and CURRENTS; with feveral other DIRECTIONS of great Advantage to this Part of Navigation in NORTH-AMERICA.

By Capt. *CYPRIAN SOUTHACK,*

Who has been Cruizing in the Service of the Crown of GREAT BRITAIN Twenty-two Years.

DIRECTIONS to Sail from the Light-houfe at Bofton in New England.

From the Light-houfe to Point ALDERTON, South by Eaft
From the Light-houfe to the South-Eaft Point of EGG Rock, Eaft half North
From the Light-houfe to Little BRUSTERS, South-Eaft, Point North Eaft, ½ Eaft
From the Light-houfe to GRAVE's Rocks, North-Eaft, ½ Eaft
From the Light-houfe to the Weftermoft Part Spit of Sand, Weft half North
From the Light-houfe to GEORGE's ISLAND, South Part, Weft half South
From the Light-houfe to RAMFORD's ISLAND, South-Eaft Part, Weft by South
From the Light-houfe to PETTIT ISLAND, North-Eaft Part, South-Weft by Weft
From the Light-houfe to CHAMBERLAIN's Point of Rocks, South-Weft half Weft
From PETTIT ISLAND, Eaft Part, to NANTASKET Road, North-Weft and by Weft
From the Light-houfe to HARDIAN's Rocks, South-Eaft, the Eaft Part
From the Light-houfe to CONIHASSET Rocks, Eaft Part, is South-Eaft and by Eaft
From the Light-houfe to St. SURREN's Rocks, Weft-South-Weft, ½ Weft
From the Light-houfe to NAHANT Rock, North by Eaft

If you come out of the Sea in the Winter Seafon, and there fhould be a great deal of Ice, my Advice is to hale a-fhore at the South Part of RAMSFORD ISLAND, on the foft Ground juft by NANTASKET Road; and there is no Ebb nor Flood will do you Damage: There ftay till you can get up to BOSTON.

For four miles, all that could be seen scattered along the beach were shattered pieces of the *Whydah* that had washed ashore. That and the bodies of more than one hundred dead pirates. Southack was also handed a report from a Justice Doane, a local official who had been among the first on the scene. According to Doane, "there had been at least 200 men from Several places at 20 miles distance plundering the Pirate Wreck of what came ashoar."

It was obvious to Southack that between the time of the sinking and his arrival at the beach, opportunistic Cape Codders, many with horses and wagons, had cleared the area of everything that could be carried away. What particularly distressed Southack was the condition of most of the pirates' bodies. Not only had the locals taken such items as shoes and pistols but rings and earrings as well, many by cutting off the pirates' fingers and ears.

More than anything else, Cyprian Southack was a stubborn and determined man. He had to admit that the great treasure that was aboard the *Whydah* was undoubtedly now lying at the bottom of the sea. But he would make certain that whatever had come ashore and had been stolen by the locals would be returned. He actually had the authority to do so. Governor Shute was willing to do almost anything to get his hands on the *Whydah*'s loot, and he had given Southack great powers. Southack could "go into any house, shop, cellar, warehouse, room or other place and in case of resistance . . . break open any door, chests, trunks" or anything else that stood in the way of his recovering plundered pirate goods.

On May 4, 1717, Southack placed an advertisement in the local newspaper stating his intentions and warning citizens that they would find themselves in the "utmost peril" if they did not cooperate with him and return whatever was in their possession that as best as he could tell had been taken from the wrecked *Whydah*. Paraphrased it read: "Whereas there is lately stranded on the back of Cape Cod a pirate ship and his Excellency the Governor has authorized me to do whatever necessary to recover any of the goods and merchandise belonging to said wreck and all of his Majesty's loving subjects are hereby commanded to be aiding and assisting me and my deputies or they will answer at the utmost peril."

Having made his intentions clear, Southack conducted a weeklong house-to-house, barn-to-barn, warehouse-to-warehouse search of a thirty-mile area. Although the locals allowed the governor's men to look wherever they pleased, Southack found absolutely nothing. Just as Cape Codders were expert at spotting shipwrecks, they were equally skilled at hiding whatever they managed to spirit away from the wrecks.

By this time, Southack was totally fed up with anyone even

A portion of Cyprian Southack's warning, in his own handwriting, that those who had concealed items from the Whydah *wreck would face dire consequences if they did not return them at once. Southack quickly learned why Cape Codders had become known for their skills at defying authority.*

remotely connected with the Cape. But he was not ready to abandon his mission. If he couldn't retrieve what had been looted from the beach, he would go after a much bigger prize. He would recover the real treasure that had gone down with the *Whydah*. Writing to Governor Shute, he informed him, "I am in Great [hope] whare the Anchors are the money is I fancy, and weather [permitting] I have Got a whale boat to fish for [it]."

Early on May 6, 1717, despite strong winds and driving rain, Southack and six of his deputies set out in his whaleboat to explore the wreck. They managed to row through the heavy surf to where he had been told the *Whydah* had gone down, where Southack hoped he might recover some of the treasure. But he was forced to admit that because of the terrible weather and "a great sea," they could "do nothing as yet."

Still, Southack refused to admit defeat. Day after day he rowed out to the spot beneath which he believed the *Whydah*, with its bags of gold and silver, lay waiting to be salvaged. Day after day he recorded the same frustration in his journal:

Monday, May 6: at Pirate Wreck this morning wind at S.E. and rain, a very great Sea on the Wreck; nothing to be done.

Tuesday, May 7: at Pirate Wreck this morning, wind at E.
Small gale & foggy, a great Sea on the Wreck. Nothing to
be done there.

Wednesday, May 8: at Pirate Wreck this morning wind
att S and fogg. Strong gale & great Sea, nothing to be
done on the Wreck.

By May 13, it had become clear, even to the determined
Southack, that the *Whydah* was in water too turbulent, too murky,
too deep, and too dangerous for him to make a recovery of its
precious cargo. As much as he hated to admit it, the mission had
been a failure. All Southack had to show for it was a collection
of timbers, cables, beams, and canvas. And he had one other
thing—a hefty bill from Eastham's town coroner for burying the
dead pirates that kept washing ashore. Outraged at being asked to
pay for these services, Southack refused to do so, which prompted
the coroner to sue him for payment. It was perhaps a fitting end to
a failed mission. Cyprian Southack, the governor's treasure seeker,
was about to go home, not only practically empty-handed, but
with a lawsuit hanging over his head.

Although the coroner's lawsuit was quickly dismissed, the

drama was still not over. At Southack's request, the vessel *Swan*, commanded by a Captain Doggett, had been commissioned to sail to Provincetown to pick up Southack, his deputies, and their meager recoveries and bring them to Boston. As it approached Cape Cod, the *Swan* was suddenly pursued, captured, and boarded by a pirate ship. After robbing Doggett of all his supplies, the pirate vessel's captain permitted him to proceed to Provincetown, where Southack was waiting.

The governor's man had not been idle, however. He had refined the journal he had kept of his misadventures. Most important, Southack, the master mapmaker, had made a map indicating the exact spot where the *Whydah* had gone down.

For locals, Southack would forever be linked with the greatest treasure that had ever made its way to the Cape. He had spent day after day rowing out to the wreck site, seeking those extraordinary riches. Had he really found nothing? they wondered. By the time Southack boarded the *Swan* for his trip home, he had become the subject of rumors that would keep the tongues of locals wagging up and down the Cape. Crafty old Southack, they told themselves and one another, had found Bellamy's gold and silver. He was about to live like a king. The hunter of plunderers, many Cape Codders were convinced, had become the greatest plunderer of them all.

CHAPTER NINE

Legends

THE STORY that Cyprian Southack had discovered a portion of the *Whydah*'s treasure and secretly spirited it away was only the first of scores of tales that would arise out of the sinking of the *Whydah*. By the end of the 1700s, there were well-known tales of the ghosts of the drowned pirates tossing coins onto the beach on stormy nights. In one of his books, published in the mid-1800s, the author Henry David Thoreau quoted an early Cape historian who wrote, "For many years after the [*Whydah*] shipwreck, a man of very singular and frightful aspect used every spring and autumn to be seen travelling on the Cape, who was supposed to have been one of Bellamy's crew. The presumption is that he went to some place where money had been secreted by the pirates, to get such a supply as [he needed]. When he died, many pieces of gold were found in a [belt] which he constantly wore."

The greatest number of stories by far were based on the legend of Sam Bellamy's relationship with Maria Hallett. According to one tale, within a few months of Sam's leaving to look for the Spanish treasure, Maria found that she was pregnant with his child. To be unmarried and pregnant in the 1700s was disgraceful and scandalous, and according to the legend, when Maria gave birth, she kept it a secret.

Then fate dealt Maria an even crueler hand. She left her baby alone in a barn for a short time, and when she returned, she found that the infant had choked to death on a piece of straw. Despite her attempts at secrecy, the townspeople of Eastham discovered what had happened and were outraged at her for having had a child out of wedlock. They began calling her bad names. The town fathers of Eastham went a step further. They put Maria in jail.

But the jail could not hold her. Time and time again, Maria escaped, which convinced the townspeople that she was a witch and had made a pact with the Devil. Each time she fled from the prison, she ran directly to the spot under the apple tree where she had first met Sam Bellamy; in another version of the tale she ran to the dunes overlooking the ocean, where she anxiously watched for the sails of Sam's ship.

Unable to keep her locked up, Eastham's town fathers released her from jail on the condition that she leave the town and never return. Fleeing to South Wellfleet, Maria built a small shack on a scraggly plot of land overlooking the ocean, known as Goody

Hallett Meadow to this day. As the story continues, things got no better for Maria in South Wellfleet. Convinced that she was a witch, no one in town would talk to her for fear that terrible things would happen to anyone who even glanced at Goody Hallett or dared walk past her shack.

There are differing versions of the lore about Maria Hallett's behavior after she settled on Goody Hallett's Meadow. In the more sympathetic stories, Maria remained loyal to Bellamy and optimistic that he would return to her, loaded with treasure, ready to marry her and take her off to their own Caribbean island. In some variations of the story, Maria, dressed in a beautiful gown she had woven herself, walked the dunes day and night, singing wild songs and constantly looking out to sea for Bellamy's returning ship. In another version, she spent the days following the wreck closely examining the body of every sailor who washed ashore, hoping he was not Sam, praying that by some miracle Sam had survived the wreck. To this day, the townspeople of Wellfleet and Eastham swear that on certain nights they can hear Maria crying out for Sam Bellamy from high atop the dunes.

Many more of the stories painted a much different picture of Maria. In these, after being shunned by those around her and feeling abandoned by Sam, Maria grew so bitter that she sold her soul to the Devil, who, in return, gave her the power to cast evil spells.

At the height of her bitterness, she conspired with the Devil and caused the storm that destroyed the *Whydah*. For days afterward, she was seen standing at the ocean's edge, head raised skyward, screaming thanks to the Devil for helping her wreak vengeance on Sam Bellamy, the man who had broken her heart.

Still other stories have grown up around Maria that are not about her relationship with Sam Bellamy. Some claim that on the night the *Whydah* went down, Maria retrieved a large chest of gold from the wreckage, which she buried in the Wellfleet dunes. But she lost her mind shortly thereafter and went to her grave having completely forgotten where she had hidden the treasure.

Even Maria's death is the subject of legend. According to one story, the townspeople of Wellfleet and Eastham became so horrified by what they believed Maria had done—and was capable of doing—that they drove her into the sea with torches and pitchforks. Even today, the people of Wellfleet insist her ghost wanders a section of town often referred to as the Devil's Pasture.

Perhaps the most fascinating of all the legends regarding the *Whydah* is the story of Black Sam Bellamy himself. As the story goes, on a spring day in 1720—three years after the wreck of the *Whydah*—a stranger went to the cemetery where Sam Bellamy and Maria Hallett had first met, lay down under the apple tree, and fell asleep. A few days later, the stranger was found there, not asleep but dead. Those who got a good look at him before he was carted off got the shock of their lives. They were absolutely convinced that the handsome young man with the long black hair was Black Sam Bellamy.

In the late 1940s, a popular New England figure named Edward Rowe Snow brought the *Whydah* back into the headlines. Snow was an author and a radio show host who was best known for a generous act he performed each December. Every Christmas, he flew his small plane along the New England coast and dropped gifts to the men and women who tended the region's lighthouses. A history buff, Snow was familiar with the story of the *Whydah*. One day, as he was flying over Eastham on one of his Christmas journeys, he looked down upon unusually clear waters and was certain he'd spotted the *Whydah* wreck. Without hesitation, he turned his plane around, swooped down low, and dropped a buoy marking the spot.

In the weeks that followed, Snow, at his own expense, constructed a fifteen-foot diving platform and had it towed to a position directly over where he thought the wreck was located. He then sent divers down in search of the *Whydah*'s treasure. The results were far from what he had hoped for. "Diver Jack Poole," he wrote, "tried his best to salvage a substantial amount of gold or silver from the wreck, but a handful of [coins] . . . was all he ever

Pirate Myths

PIRATES, who have been and remain among the most popular and most colorful figures in literature and on the movie screen, have been surrounded by misconceptions since their heyday in the late seventeenth and early eighteenth centuries. Three conceptions in particular that have been widely believed are in fact substantially false.

The first is the notion that pirates buried their treasure and then drew maps indicating where it lay hidden. The truth is that most pirates didn't hold on to their loot long enough to bury it. Many gambled or drank it away. Others spent it in pirate havens such as New Providence, in the Bahamas, and Port Royal, in Jamaica, in shops especially established to relieve them of the money they had stolen. Also, much of the pirates' booty was not gold or silver or jewels but ordinary trade goods, such as lumber, cloth, and animal hides—all items that would have been ruined if they had been buried.

So where did the notion of pirates' buried treasure come from? It was established in the pages of popular nineteenth- and early-twentieth-century books such as Robert Louis Stevenson's *Treasure Island*, and it has been kept alive in stories that feature the search for buried treasure as an integral part of their plot, from the novel *Swallows and Amazons* by Arthur Ransome in 1930 to movies such as *Pirates of the Caribbean*.

Another myth, almost as popular as they myth of buried treasure, claims that pirates made their victims walk the plank. Pirates were not above torturing their victims, but there is not a shred of evidence that any pirate crew made someone walk the plank. As one pirate historian has noted, why make victims walk the plank when it's easier to just throw them overboard?

The third popular pirate myth concerns how they spoke. Thanks once again to movies made from the novel *Treasure Island* and other pirate stories, we've been led to believe that such expressions as "Shiver me timbers," "Ahoy, matey," and "Arrrrrr" were staples of what has been termed "pirate speak." It's simply not true. Given their origins, most pirates spoke the same way that all lower-class sailors from England, Scotland, Wales, and the American colonies spoke at the time. It is interesting that one man can be credited for having created the fictitious pirate speak — the British actor Robert Newton. In 1950, he played Long John Silver in the movie version of *Treasure Island*, and went on to play him in a television series in which he popularized the accent and many of the sayings that are commonly associated with pirates today.

brought to the surface. We almost lost one boy by drowning when he attempted to swim ashore from the platform at high tide, and then a terrific storm hit which smashed the platform to pieces."

Eventually it would be discovered that the wreck Snow had probed was not the *Whydah* but another victim of the sea. But the warning that Snow issued after his experience still held true. "It will be a very lucky treasure hunter," he cautioned, "who ever does more than pay expenses while attempting to find the elusive gold and silver still aboard the *Whydah*. . . . The great billows which constantly break at this part of the coast will cause all but the most determined treasure seekers to give up in despair after a few hours of being battered and tossed by the [waves] of Wellfleet."

CHAPTER TEN

The Search for the Whydah

WHEN I WAS VERY YOUNG," historian Arthur T. Vanderbilt wrote some fifty years after Snow issued his warning, "my grandfather told me the story of the pirate ship *Whydah*. For many summers thereafter, I walked Cape Cod's outer beach, looking not for smoothed pebbles or flawless shells, but for pieces of eight. On winter nights when the wind roared under the eaves like the surf booming along the coast, I dreamed of finding a doubloon gleaming in the wet sand, the first of a cache of coins the waves would wash about my feet."

The story of the pirate ship *Whydah* might well have ended with its sinking had it not been for Martha's Vineyard real-estate developer, builder, and salvage company owner Barry Clifford. His real passion, however, was something else again. In whatever spare time he could manage, he dove the waters off Cape Cod and the Vineyard, looking for sunken ships.

As he was growing up on Cape Cod, one of the things Clifford most loved to do was listen to his uncle Bill tell him stories about Cape Cod shipwrecks, pirate ships, and sunken treasure. His favorite tale was about the *Whydah*. He could not understand how a ship containing so much gold, silver, ivory, and precious jewels could remain undiscovered for almost three hundred years.

The older Clifford got, the more intense his interest in the *Whydah* became. On November 7, 1982, at the age of thirty-seven, he announced that he was going to devote himself to finding the pirate ship.

He began his quest in libraries, seeking what little information existed about exactly where the *Whydah* had sunk beneath the waves. He read every newspaper account of the shipwreck, but his most valuable resources by far were the letters, journals, and maps of Cyprian Southack. According to Clifford, finding these documents was like discovering a compass to the wreck site. "He told us where the ship was and why he couldn't get to it," Clifford explained. Nothing was more useful than the map that Southack had drawn of the waters off Eastham and Wellfleet, particularly the two miles of ocean surrounding the spot that Southack had labeled *"The Pirate Ship Whido Lost."*

Coming close to the importance of Southack's map were two entries in his journal. In one of them he had noted (as paraphrased), "At 5 in the morning the English man [Thomas Davis] that was

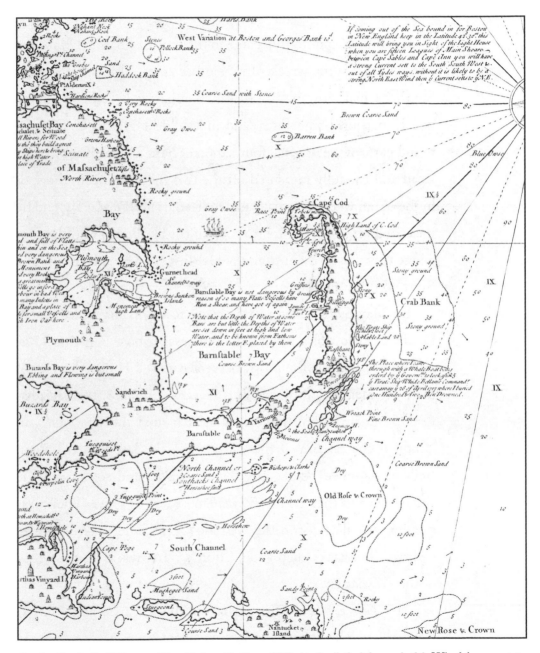

Cyprian Southack's 1717 map of Cape Cod, used by Barry Clifford to finally find the wreck of the Whydah, *was a typical example of his map-making skills in both its accuracy and the amount of detail it provided about various locations.*

saved out of the pirate ship came to the house of Samuel Harding, two miles from the wreck." In the other entry (also paraphrased), Southack had written that it was "3 miles ½ by land from the wreck to Billingsgate [an island in Wellfleet Harbor]." Clifford found parts of the original foundation of Samuel Harding's homestead and carefully measured off the two miles to locate the spot in the ocean where Southack had indicated the *Whydah* lay, and he measured off the 3½ miles from Wellfleet Harbor to find the spot where the measurement from the Harding homestead and the one from Wellfleet Harbor met.

By May 1983, Clifford was ready to begin his active search for the long-lost pirate ship. He purchased a boat he named *Vast Explorer* to serve as the project's surface vessel. He and several of his crew members took the *Vast Explorer* offshore, then headed farther out in a small motorized skiff named the *Crumpstey,* in honor of the captain of the *Mary Anne,* the last ship that Sam Bellamy captured before meeting the *Fisher* and setting off the chain of events that led the *Whydah* to its watery grave. Their destination was the spot in the Atlantic Ocean where, according to Cyprian Southack's map and Clifford's other research, the wreck of the *Whydah* lay.

The *Vast Explorer*'s first mate for the summer was John F. Kennedy Jr. The son of the late president, twenty-two-year-old

Barry Clifford and members of his team aboard the surface vessel the Vast Explorer. *Together, the team has salvaged more than 100,000 artifacts from the* Whydah *shipwreck.*

Kennedy was on summer vacation from Brown University. He had met Clifford on Martha's Vineyard and had become fascinated with both the story of the *Whydah* and the search for its remains. He was particularly taken with Clifford's unwavering conviction that he would find the pirate ship. "That optimism," Kennedy stated, "spreads to everyone. We started talking about diving, and through a shared interest in it we became friends. He was telling me about the *Whydah,* and he said, 'If you want to do some diving, that's fine.' How often do you get to do something like dive a shipwreck?"

At first, some members of the crew were concerned that the young member of a rich and famous family would not work as hard as he needed to. "When I told [one of my crew members] JFK Jr. was going to be on the crew," Clifford later recalled, "he frowned and demanded, 'Is he bringing his butler with him? What am I supposed to do with a Kennedy?'" The crewman needn't have worried. John Kennedy Jr. would prove to be one of the hardest workers involved in the *Whydah* search.

Clifford was able to attract quality crew with varied experience. They were a diverse lot, united by a passion for the sea, a love of adventure, and the lure of sunken treasure. The first to join the team was a six-foot-ten veteran fisherman named Richard "Stretch" Grey. He was followed by John Beyer, who was already working for Clifford at his salvage company. The majority of Expedition Whydah's crew were friends that Clifford had made in college some twenty years ago. They included his former roommate Robert McClung; retired Colorado judge John Levin; Bill Dibble, a former Marine jet pilot who had flown more than one hundred missions over Vietnam; and motorcycle racer and rodeo rider Trip Wheeler; and Todd Murphy, who served with the Green Beret's combat scuba team.

Along with his full-time crew, Clifford recruited several respected marine archaeologists to serve as consultants to his project. And he scored a real coup by persuading renowned underwater-treasure seeker Mel Fisher to participate as well. Fisher had found and recovered the remainder of the treasure aboard the Spanish fleet that had sunk off the Florida coast in 1715 — the same sunken fleet that Sam Bellamy had gone looking for before becoming a pirate. Fisher won even greater glory when, after aiding Clifford and his team, he discovered and salvaged the Spanish galleon *Nuestra Señora de Atocha*, which had sunk in 1622. Before salvaging operations were completed, an astounding $450 million in treasure was recovered from that ship.

Clifford was well aware of the enormous challenges that he faced as he began his physical search for the *Whydah*. Bellamy's ship had gone down in some of the most turbulent waters off

North America. The weather off Cape Cod would permit a search for the vessel for only a few months a year. And given the nature of the ocean floor in the area where the *Whydah* had met its fate, the vessel was bound to be buried under an untold number of feet of sand that, after more than 265 years, was certain to have shifted considerably.

On the other hand, Clifford was aware that searching for shipwrecks, no matter how old, had changed dramatically since the days when Cyprian Southack had peered over the side of his small open boat, hoping to get a glimpse of the *Whydah* and its treasure below. Thanks to technical advancements that in many cases had been made on behalf of military navigation or oil exploration, underwater electronic equipment had reached a point where, as one marine archaeologist put it, "our ability to observe the ocean environment . . . has finally caught up with our imaginations."

In the *Crumpstey* that first day, Clifford and his crew carried a heavy torpedo-shaped device called a magnetometer. Invented in 1833 by German mathematician Carl Friedrich Gauss, a magnetometer can detect the presence of iron or steel, no matter how far below the surface it lies, and then record it as a "hit" on a graph. Having received almost two centuries of constant improvements, the magnetometer is considered the most effective instrument for locating sunken objects.

The divers searching for Whydah *artifacts have been forced to work in dark, churning waters. Here, team diver Chris Macort uses a lamp and a metal detector to guide him to small items such as jewelry and coins.*

Clifford and the crew spent more than three weeks carrying out extensive electronic surveying with their magnetometer, charting wherever they received a hit. At the end of that time, they had received about 150 scattered hits. Hoping they'd identified the location of the wreck, they then brought the *Vast Explorer* to a spot directly over where they had recorded the largest number of responses and dropped four large anchors to make sure their vessel held its position.

As their work continued, the Expedition Whydah team also used bottom-penetrating sonar to send out sound waves in search of buried artifacts from the ship. With sonar technology, sound waves bounce back like echoes when they encounter hard objects. A computer measures the time it takes for the sound waves and their echoes to return from the object they struck and calculates the distance between the sonar transceiver and the object. By using a series of these pings, the computer can create a picture of the object, revealing its shape and size and how far it lies beneath the sand.

The beginning of Clifford's search for the *Whydah* included not only the use of magnetometer and sonar technology but also the introduction of a practice that involved the use of what he and his team termed a "mailbox." They took two huge aluminum pipe elbows and placed them over the *Vast Explorer*'s dual propellers at the back of the vessel. They angled the pipes down so that, when the engines were revved, the powerful wash from the propellers that was directed toward the ocean floor would shove sand aside to form a crater or pit. By doing so directly above the location they'd identified as the most promising, they hoped to expose the *Whydah*'s coveted artifacts and treasures.

Finally, it was time to dive down and examine the pits. Crew members sifted through the locations of large hits, hoping to find cannons or clustered cannonballs. They dug in and around the places where small hits had been recorded, thinking there might be smaller objects such as coins or jewelry or other personal items. Clifford and his divers used relatively newly developed electronic-ranging devices that sent out radio signals from marked spots so that they could return each day to within three feet of where they had been exploring the previous day.

Several of the large hits turned out to be metal sections or iron rods from the radio towers of a Marconi transatlantic wireless station that had been thrown into the sea off Wellfleet when the station was abandoned in 1920. Other hits, large and small, were World War II–era objects, such as bullets, shell casings, and practice bombs left behind by the Army Air Corps, which used the waters off Wellfleet to conduct training exercises. One such discovery provided the team with its first dramatic moment. Early on,

Diving

ACCORDING TO OFFICIALS of the National Oceanic and Atmospheric Administration, "The suite of tools available [to probe the ocean floor and search for shipwrecks] would amaze the ocean explorers of yesteryear." These tools include such technological marvels as small manned submarines called submersibles; unmanned, remotely operated underwater vehicles known as ROVs; sophisticated sounding devices; and high-intensity lighting and high-resolution imaging techniques, the equivalent of a microscope for researchers examining what lies in the deep sea. While those searching for the *Whydah* have taken advantage of these technological marvels, they also believe that there is nothing more important when examining the time capsule that is a shipwreck than a human being conducting a hands-on search by diving down to the site of the wreck.

Diving is an ancient endeavor. Artifacts reveal that as long as 4,500 years ago, people from Mesopotamia, breathing through hollow reeds, dove down to the ocean floor in search of pearl oysters. About two hundred years later, Greek sponge divers began to dive for one of the world's most useful naturally growing products and coincidentally discovered a number of history's oldest shipwrecks.

The methods used by early divers were extremely limited in terms of both depth and the time they could remain underwater. Arguably the most famous of all the earliest dives took place in 332 BCE, when, during the siege of the city of Tyre, in Lebanon, Alexander the Great,

In this medieval painting, Alexander the Great, one of the earliest proponents of underwater exploration, is shown being lowered into the Mediterranean in a glass diving barrel.

in a forerunner to the diving bell, dove down in a "very fine barrel made entirely of white glass," to observe obstructions that had been placed at the bottom of the city's harbor.

Beginning in the late 1500s, great breakthroughs were made in diving equipment. The earliest was the development of an effective diving bell, an open-bottomed container that is large enough to hold a person. Once the bell is lowered to the ocean floor, the intense pressure of the water keeps air trapped within the bell, allowing its user to breathe. A window on the side of the bell affords the occupant a limited view of the surroundings. In 1686, William Phips used a diving bell to discover the huge fortune from a sunken Spanish treasure ship that he recovered off the island of Haiti. Phips's accomplishment inspired legions of future adventurers, including Sam Bellamy and Paulsgrave Williams in 1715, to seek instant riches at the bottom of the sea.

Effective diving suits began to appear in the early 1700s. One of the first was introduced by Andrew Becker and consisted of a leather-covered suit, a helmet that included a window, and a system of tubes extending to the surface for air. In the 1830s, Augustus Siebe improved upon Becker's creation by building a diving suit featuring a helmet fitted to a full-length watertight canvas garment. Beginning in the late 1800s, most diving suits were made of a solid sheet of rubber between layers of twill.

The man who brought the world of diving into the modern era was the French oceanographer, inventor, researcher, and filmmaker Jacques-Yves Cousteau. Between 1942 and 1943, Cousteau, with his partner Emile Gagnan, invented the Aqua-Lung, a self-contained underwater breathing apparatus (SCUBA) that featured a demand regulator to supply divers with compressed air. Not only did the Aqua-Lung revolutionize diving by making it possible for those who explore and salvage shipwrecks to conduct their operations more "up close and personal" than ever before; it also opened the door to recreational diving for millions of people.

Extraordinary tools of underwater exploration continue to be invented. In 2014, the world was introduced to what can legitimately be called the most amazing form of diving apparatus yet. Called an Exosuit, it is a diving outfit that weighs 530 pounds, can dive to depths of one thousand feet, and can remain underwater for approximately fifty hours — deeper and longer than is possible with even the best conventional scuba gear. Prior to the development of the Exosuit, only submersibles could reach those depths and maintain them for so long, but the Exosuit contains 1.6-horsepower foot-controlled thrusters and eighteen rotary joints in its arms and legs to provide its user with a freedom of movement far greater than can be achieved in even the most nimble submersible.

one of the divers returned to the *Vast Explorer* thrilled by a cylindrical object that he had found. Holding the object over his head, he shouted, "I think it's a small cannon." To which Todd Murphy, the only person present who had served in the military, shouted, "Throw it back! That's a bomb!" The diver did throw it back, and fortunately, after an examination by an explosives expert, it was determined that the underwater device was a harmless World War II dummy practice bomb.

Finally, on August 4, 1983, underneath about ten feet of sand in one of the first pits that had been dug, team members discovered a ship's rudder strap, a section of rigging from a mast, bronze chisel-point nails, and firebrick from a vessel. These finds were not bags of coins or anything with the *Whydah*'s name or other identifying marks on them, but Clifford and his men were convinced they were from the *Whydah*. In what Clifford would later describe as "that first, terribly dry season . . . it was a ray of hope that they were at least searching in the right place."

CHAPTER ELEVEN

Victory at Last

FOR THE EXPEDITION WHYDAH CREW, the winter and early spring of 1983–1984 seemed to drag on forever. Well past April 1984, the weather was too harsh and the ocean was too turbulent for the group to consider diving. Finally, in late May, the weather turned calm enough for the expedition's second season to begin. But try as they might, Clifford and his men spent the next two months experiencing the same frustrations and lack of success that they had the previous season. Again the only things their dives netted them were reminders of World War II training drills and sections of the Marconi towers. Even more serious, they were running out of money. Clifford was all too aware that unless something dramatic enough to attract additional investors took place—and soon—the entire project was in jeopardy.

Adding to Clifford's problems was the prospect of being embarrassed before millions of viewers on national television. Filled with optimism when the season began, he had invited nationally known television reporter Nancy Fernandes to bring her NBC crew out to the *Vast Explorer* to film the progress he was certain Expedition Whydah would be making by then. Now, with his artifact lockers still almost completely empty, he dreaded the film crew's arrival.

When Fernandes and her crew climbed aboard on July 20, Clifford, anxious to postpone the disaster for as long as possible, had them transferred to the *Crumpstey* and taken on a whale watch. But he could not continue to delay the inevitable. When they returned to the *Vast Explorer,* Clifford had the mailboxes blast out a twenty-foot pit. Then he sent down a diver named Mike Kacergis, who had just joined the team, to investigate. As Clifford would later admit, if the television crew had not been there, he would probably not have conducted any explorations that day. Kacergis, Clifford would recount, "was young and excited and ready for action. The rest of us were tired, burned out, and somewhat cynical. It was probably the fiftieth hole we had blown and examined since the excavation started. None had contained artifacts. We expected the same would be true of this hole, too."

But he was wrong. Within a short time, Kacergis was back up on deck. With the television cameras rolling, he tore out his mouthpiece and shouted, "Hey, you guys! There's three cannons down there!"

Clifford was suffering from an ear problem incurred on a

The storm that sunk the Whydah *broke the ship apart, scattering it over the ocean floor. Here, an Expedition* Whydah *diver locates part of the ship and prepares to have it hoisted to the surface.*

previous dive, but he quickly sent others down to the pit. And they could not believe their eyes. There lay cannons, musket balls, a rusty cutlass, a flintlock pistol, and a shoe with, as one of the searchers described it, "toe prints still in the leather." Scattered around the pit were small, flat, encrusted objects that gave promise of being coins.

The team members returned to the *Vast Explorer*, bringing one of the smaller objects and what appeared to be a cannonball up with them. When the incrustations covering the round object were removed, a cannonball from the *Whydah* era was indeed revealed. While others worked on the cannonball, Clifford carefully chipped away at the small, flat object. "At first," he later wrote, "I'd thought it was an odd-shaped shell. But as I succeeded in loosening it, I could see it wasn't. I held the coin in my hand and flipped it over. There was a silver cross on it and clearly visible, a date: 1684."

"This artifact," Clifford stated, "represented only a beginning for us. Still, July 20, 1984, was a heady day for us. From now on we knew that we were digging in the right area and could actually start finding the things we had come for. We passed around the cannonball and coin for several hours, elated at having found an authentic piece of the *Whydah*."

The objects recovered on July 20 were indeed "only a beginning." Buoyed by their initial discoveries, and with their morale fully restored, the Expedition Whydah team spent the next five months working harder than ever, blasting pits, diving down, examining the pits, and retrieving the artifacts they discovered.

In early December 1984, Clifford held a press conference. And he had much to report. Since the first discoveries in July, the team had uncovered and retrieved a treasure trove. One pit alone had yielded, among other items, more than three thousand silver coins from the Spanish Empire; four gold coins, each worth $40,000; and gold and silver jewelry. From another pit, Clifford reported, his crew had recovered four cannons, an eight-foot-long anchor, gold bars, a silver bar, silver coins, gold dust, and brass shoe buckles.

True to his flair for the dramatic, Clifford dumped many of the coins out on a wooden table and said, "Imagine the sound of these down in the bilge when [the pirates] counted them." He concluded the press conference by stating, "If we dug seven and a half test pits a day it would take the next ten years to complete the excavation. They probably had ten tons of treasure on this thing. We have barely scratched the surface."

They had indeed hardly begun the excavation process. And they had another challenge as well. Exciting though the second season's discoveries were, not one of the artifacts they had recovered offered proof that it had come from the *Whydah*. Jim Bradley, a member of both the Massachusetts Historical Commission and

Barry Clifford displays coins retrieved from the Whydah.

the Massachusetts Board of Underwater Archaeological Resources, echoed the sentiments of many of those unwilling to declare that the *Whydah* had been found. Speaking of what Clifford and his team had discovered on July 24, 1984, he said, "It's an early wreck, it's an important wreck, it has some of the same characteristics as the *Whydah* may have. But to say it's the *Whydah* is premature at least. That area of the Cape has one of the highest densities of shipwrecks of any place on the East Coast. There are hundreds and hundreds of wrecks out there."

It was frustrating for Clifford and his crew, to say the least. The Expedition Whydah team had recovered millions of dollars' worth of coins, gold dust, and other artifacts. But Jim Bradley was right. They still had not been able to find any proof that what they were recovering was coming from the *Whydah*. And those who doubted it were becoming increasingly vocal.

With both fall and the end of the 1985 diving season rapidly approaching, Clifford decided to act on a hunch. Not far from where the first cannon had been found, the magnetometer had registered a large hit. Knowing that it would probably be the last major effort of the season, he ordered that a large pit be blown at that spot, and he sent Robert McClung down to investigate. Here again, Expedition Whydah would benefit from the ever-increasing sophistication of the technology that accompanied their underwater search. McClung was hooked up to a system that used a microphone and earphones to communicate directly with Clifford and the rest of his team on the *Vast Explorer*.

Anxious minutes passed before McClung's voice broke through loud and clear. "There's something huge down here," he shouted, "but I can't tell what it is."

"Maybe it's a rock and you just don't recognize it," someone from the team responded.

"I don't think so," McClung replied. "I think it's a bell."

Knowing that almost every ship of the 1600s and 1700s had a large bell on which its name was inscribed, Clifford donned his diving gear and joined McClung. As soon as he arrived at the site, it was clear to him that the object was indeed a bell. "My heart began to trip," he later recalled. "I kicked down and tried to rub the side of it clean to see if there was a name etched in its cast-bronze sides. The metal was heavily [covered with layers of ocean matter], and I couldn't tell what ship it was from."

At that point, as the excitement was building among those on the *Vast Explorer*, Bob Cembrola, a visiting archaeologist, dove down to measure the object and map its location. Returning to the surface, Cembrola, also convinced that it was a bell, declared, "It looks like the right bell. It is definitely eighteenth century. . . . But I don't know if it's from the *Whydah*." Within days it was hauled to the surface by heavy straps wrapped around it and taken to the laboratory, where it was placed in a tank filled with water. An electric current in the tank was used to break the incrustations away from the bell.

"I tried not to think about the bell after that," Clifford remembers. "For one thing, it might not have been the *Whydah*'s, or it might have been a bell from one of the ships that the pirates robbed. Another reason not to think about the bell was the incrustations that covered it. Sometimes it takes months or even years for incrustations to fall away. You can hurry them a little, especially if they are loose, but usually you want to wait until they are ready to fall off before doing any chipping. That way you avoid damaging an artifact."

Fortunately for Clifford and his team, they did not have to wait months or years. Some three weeks after the bell had been placed in the laboratory tank, a large chunk of incrustation fell off, revealing the word "Gally," a common colonial-era spelling of "Galley." The excitement in the lab rose to fever pitch. As the team gathered around them, Carl Becker and some of the lab's other conservationists began carefully scraping away the rest of the incrustation with dental picks. After about twenty minutes, a Maltese cross and the date 1716 were revealed. Then a much larger chunk of incrustation fell away. And there before them on the side of the bell were the words they had prayed would be there:

THE WHYDAH GALLY 1716

The news spread almost immediately, and scores of people, many from the archaeological world, rushed to view what had been found. Among them was Joseph A. Sinnott, director of the Massachusetts Board of Underwater Archaeological Resources, the agency responsible for monitoring Clifford's salvage efforts. Stating that the discovery of the bell removed all doubt about the ship's identity, Sinnott proclaimed, "I don't think you could hope for more." Even those archaeologists and other individuals who had previously refused to believe that Clifford had found the *Whydah* had to publicly admit that the first-ever pirate shipwreck to be found had been authenticated beyond any question.

The discovery of the bell and its inscription brought about another result as well. Until that development, the Clifford team had assumed that the name of the ship they were searching for was spelled "Whidah." That's the way it was spelled in Defoe's *General History of the Pyrates* and almost every other contemporary account.

"I guess I'll have to change all of the stationery," team member Todd Murphy declared.

Barry Clifford with the most important artifact recovered from the Whydah.

Preserving the Artifacts

SEARCHING FOR, discovering, and excavating the artifacts that accompany shipwrecks like the *Whydah* are exciting and highly publicized endeavors. But the slower and less-reported efforts to conserve what is retrieved from these wrecks provide immense value to the historical record. Conservation is the process of stabilizing and protecting historical artifacts. It is not the goal of conservators to restore artifacts to their original condition. Rather, it is to preserve an object in its present condition and to stop any further deterioration.

Each type of material, be it wood, metal, leather, or cloth, requires a specific treatment in order to preserve it. Over the years, scientists and conservators have developed and improved methods and techniques to make their preservation efforts more effective and longer-lasting.

As the Expedition Whydah team can attest, many of the artifacts that have gone down with ships and lain for years at the bottom of the sea are embedded in concretions—chunks of rock, clay, and sand that are cemented together through chemical reactions that take place over time in seawater. As long as concretions remain covered in salt water, any objects within them will remain stable. But if a concretion, once brought to the surface, is allowed to dry out, its artifacts will quickly deteriorate unless they are preserved.

When an artifact covered in concretions is brought to the surface, it is quickly X-rayed to discover what lies inside. Mobile digital X-ray technology, a kind of X-ray room on wheels, makes it possible to get a clear image of what is hidden within the concretions. If X-rays reveal artifacts, the entire mass of cemented material is taken to a conservation laboratory and immediately placed in a tank of water that, in order to avoid exposing

Two preservationists work on a sail that has been recovered from the ocean floor.

the material to contaminants, is as pure and fresh as possible. Some four weeks later, it is moved to a tank containing a chemical solution designed to make it easier to get at whatever items may be inside. After the material has soaked for two or three days, a low-voltage electric current is applied in order to encourage the mass of rock, clay, and sand to fall away from the objects inside. Then conservationists painstakingly remove any incrustations that remain, using picks and brushes. Finally, the artifacts are washed and dried, and a protective coating called a sealant is applied to them.

This long process is nothing compared with some other conservation efforts, such as the preservation of the entire hull of King Henry VIII's flagship *Mary Rose*, which sank in 1545 and was brought to the surface in 1982. In order to preserve this historic treasure, conservators at the Mary Rose Museum continually sprayed the hull with water for twelve years and then sprayed it with a preservative called polyethylene glycol (PEG) for another nineteen years. Today, the *Mary Rose* remains one of the world's greatest historical treasures.

"Not to mention all of the T-shirts and caps," Clifford responded.

Team member Tuck Whitaker had a bigger problem. "Forget that stuff," he said, pointing to his chest. "I have to change my tattoo."

As Clifford and his team knew from the start, excavating the *Whydah* would always be a seasonal affair. Only in the late spring, summer, and early fall are oceanic and climatic conditions good enough to allow for an effective search. Still, millions of dollars in silver and gold coins, gold bars, gold dust, hand guns, pewter tableware, and other artifacts, including thirty cannons, have been recovered. For members of the team, including the pirate historian Ken Kinkor, each discovery had a meaning well beyond its monetary value. "Look at these," Kinkor once exclaimed as he held a pile of gold coins in his hand. "The last time a human touched them, they were either being handled by a pirate—or being used to buy human lives."

"On July 19, 1998," Barry Clifford wrote, "we discovered the hull of the *Whydah*. In all the years I had been digging on this site, discovering the actual vessel that held Bellamy and his crew ranks as the most exciting of all finds, even more so than the discovery of the ship's bell or the finding of the first bar of gold. This was, after all, the ship itself, a significant piece of the vessel that allowed the world of Bellamy and his pirates to exist."

Even more exciting to Barry Clifford and his team than the discovery of Whydah *treasure and artifacts has been the discovery of sections and pieces of the ship itself. Here, a diver examines a lead-lined piece of the pirate ship's gunpowder room.*

Expedition Whydah has now been under way for more than thirty years. Each diving season has resulted in the discovery and retrieval of thousands of artifacts that increase our knowledge of the *Whydah*'s history and dramatically alter our perception of pirates and their way of life. Yet with all that has been accomplished, Clifford and the archaeologists who serve as his consultants are convinced that there are still many artifacts waiting to be discovered, perhaps including priceless seventeenth- and early-eighteenth-century art objects, additional sections of the *Whydah*'s hull, and personal items from both the ship's crew and the people they robbed. There is no way of knowing how long one of the most fascinating and productive of all nautical archaeological endeavors will continue.

Furthermore, despite the thousands of coins that have been salvaged, the vast bulk of the more than four hundred thousand coins that the *Whydah*'s survivors swore were aboard the ship when it went down still remains to be discovered. "To think," Clifford stated more than ten years ago, "that we have found only a small portion of the *Whydah* treasure gives me pause. The two hundred thousand artifacts we have already found have caused a bursting at the seams at our conservation lab. Yet how can we stop?"

CHAPTER TWELVE

What the Artifacts Tell Us

THE ARTIFACTS that continue to be recovered from the *Whydah* are both unique and revealing, made even more so by the fact that, thanks to the extraordinary number of ships that Sam Bellamy plundered, they come from at least twelve countries on four continents. As Ken Kinkor stated, "Each shipwreck is a time capsule, and each artifact from the *Whydah* has its own story to tell about what pirates were really like and what life was like on April 26, 1717."

For example, the huge quantity of stylish white shirts, satin, silk, and velvet britches, embroidered vests, expensive cuff links, silver buckles, brass buttons, and neck chains found on the ocean floor around the *Whydah* reveal that the pirates were far more fashionable, even dandyish, in their dress than previously believed. Historians have concluded that the wearing of these items, presumably taken from wealthy passengers aboard the ships they looted, was an act of defiance against the rigid class hierarchy

A member of the Expedition Whydah team works to preserve a grindstone brought up from the wreck.

of the day in which only the upper class dressed in such elegant fashion.

Sailors on seventeenth- and eighteenth-century navy and merchant ships spent mealtimes sharing a bucket of meat and a tray of biscuits among a group of up to nine men. The only utensil these sailors had was their personal knife, the same one they used in battle. They would dip a biscuit into the bucket, scoop out some meat and some juice, and eat it. There was no such thing as plates aboard.

Up until the artifacts from the *Whydah* began to be uncovered, that crude method of dining was thought to be typical on pirate vessels as well. However, forks, spoons, knives, and, most interestingly, pewter plates, inscribed with the initials of members of the *Whydah*'s crew, tell us that the pirates not only dressed better than common sailors, they also ate in a different, more sophisticated manner than had previously been known and has commonly been portrayed.

The *Whydah* pirates enjoyed a far more varied diet than the sailors on merchant or navy ships. Perhaps this should not be surprising, since the booty on the *Whydah* included foodstuffs taken from ships carrying cargo that originated in many different countries. Items brought up from the *Whydah* site also disclose that the pirates' meals included such items as fish, turtles, and birds that they caught.

If one were to believe the depictions of pirates in books, movies, and television, one would expect the most common objects salvaged from the *Whydah* to be eye patches, bottles of rum, and perhaps even the remains of parrots. The truth, however, is that the most common items of all have been musket balls, shotgun pellets, and homemade baseball-size hand grenades, all designed to force into surrender the ships they boarded and to subdue those who dared put up a fight.

Historians and archaeologists have been particularly surprised by the inscriptions on a large number of wax seals that continue to be found near the wreck. Because many of the pirates, like millions of other people of their day, could neither read nor write, they signed documents, such as the Articles of Agreement, using a stamplike device called a seal. Often the seals contained their initials, but they might also bear images and symbols that said something about their owner's personality. A significant number of the seals recovered from the *Whydah* express love, hope, or desire, sentiments that have not often been associated with individuals who are more often described as "thuggish white men with sabers." Many archaeologists regard seals as invaluable in helping us understand an emotional side of pirates that had not been revealed previously.

Medical syringes were another startling discovery among the *Whydah*'s artifacts. In an age when medical knowledge and practice were primitive at best, the syringes represent a degree of medical sophistication not previously thought to exist among pirates.

A syringe was among the pieces of sophisticated medical equipment at the disposal of the Whydah's *doctor, James Ferguson.*

The finest treasure found at the wreckage site is gold jewelry made by the Akan, a people native to what is today Ghana and the Ivory Coast, in west Africa. At the time the *Whydah* was capturing and looting ship after ship, Akan jewelry was being traded in Africa and sold in Europe. The pieces of Akan jewelry recovered from the *Whydah* are of particularly great value and interest to anthropologists and historians because experts have determined that they are the oldest examples of this type of jewelry ever found.

Members of the Expedition Whydah team have also retrieved a significant number of gold bars. The gold bars have all been scored with a knife, indicating that either Bellamy's men or the captain of the ship that originally traded for the bars wanted to make sure that they were solid gold and not lead with a gold coating. The silver bars found in the *Whydah* wreckage were made by the pirates themselves by melting down various types of silver objects from their booty. Turning looted silver and gold into bars made them easier to carry and, more important, easier to divide among the crew.

Then there are the coins, the essence of any pirate treasure. Although the Expedition Whydah's crew has not yet been able to find anywhere near the four hundred thousand coins the ship was purported to be carrying, a small fortune in coins has been recovered. And, aside from their monetary value, they are special.

"In twenty minutes one day," Clifford recalls, "I found 280 coins. They weighed almost twenty pounds. I could have tied them to a line and raised them that way, but I did not want them to leave my hands. These coins were the heart and soul of the *Whydah* and the primary reason that her pirates had become pirates. I wanted to hold them close for the secrets they could tell me." To Clifford, holding them close has not meant keeping them in his personal possession. Almost all the artifacts recovered from the *Whydah* thus far, including almost all the coins, are on display in the Whydah Pirate Museum that Clifford established in Provincetown, on Cape Cod.

Of all the *Whydah* artifacts recovered thus far, none has captured more attention than a leg bone with a small black leather shoe and a silk stocking still attached to it. When these objects were found, Clifford was convinced that they had belonged to a very small adult pirate. "I had been looking at this shoe and thinking, 'My God, these people were really small back then,'" Clifford recalled. Ken Kinkor, however, had a different idea and persuaded Clifford to have the items tested.

After analyzing the leg bone, shoe, and stocking, John de Bry, director of the Center for Historical Archaeology, and the Smithsonian Institution anthropologist David R. Hunt came to the conclusion that they had belonged not to a small man but to a boy between eight and eleven years old. To both Clifford and Kinkor, their finding made perfect sense. The leg bone, shoe, and stocking most likely belonged to John King, the rebellious youth who had defied his mother by joining the pirates.

There is no question that Barry Clifford and his team's achievements in the face of hostile seas and shifting sands have been major. And they have had to deal with another significant obstacle as well. From the time that the excavation of the *Whydah* began, Clifford has been the subject of criticism from members of the scientific community who accuse him of being a treasure hunter primarily interested in acquiring riches rather than a serious marine archaeologist concerned with recovering artifacts to add to our knowledge of what took place in the past.

Clifford has attempted to counter this criticism by pointing out that from the beginning his team has included several respected marine archaeologists who have served as advisers to the project, and that rather than sell the treasure he has recovered, he has placed it in a museum to be shared with the public. "I [am] not a treasure hunter," Clifford has stated, "although I [am] obviously hunting for treasure. I [am] a history hunter, an undersea salvor with a driving interest in bringing a great historic period back to life in a responsible way that a working man could appreciate as well as a historian."

Coins: Windows to the Past

OF ALL THE VARIOUS TYPES of artifacts that open up windows to what has gone on before us, none are more revealing than coins. Archaeologists who study coins regard them as a vital source of information about the history, the ways of life, the values, and the cultures of the past, along with how art, religion, music, dance, and myths have helped shape societies. Coins tell us so much about the past that they have been called both "newspapers in metal" and "miniature libraries of history." At a time before the rise and spread of newspapers, radio, magazines, and other forms of media, kings, emperors, and governments used the depictions they engraved on their coins to celebrate or commemorate events, honor individuals, or otherwise spread their messages.

Depictions engraved on coins, including those recovered from the *Whydah*, tell us much about the men and women who ruled at the time the coins were made — what these rulers looked like, how they dressed, and even, on some coins, their favorite possessions. A significant number of the Spanish coins recovered from the *Whydah* depict the powerful Spanish monarch Charles V, who ruled over an empire so huge that he proudly and correctly declared that the sun never set upon it.

Other excavated coins tell us about the heroes of their day. For example, a 1691 French coin found in the wreckage of the *Whydah*, minted during the reign of Louis XIV, depicts the achievements of William Dampier, an English buccaneer and explorer who, in the very year that

A small portion of the gold doubloons, silver reals, and gold and silver ingots that have been brought up from the **Whydah**. *Hundreds of millions of dollars of loot, particularly more coins, remain to be found.*

the coin was made, became the first person to circumnavigate the globe twice. Dampier would go on to achieve a third circumnavigation in 1710.

One of the most important ways that coins contribute to our knowledge of the past is through the engravings of buildings and landmarks that often appear on them. For archaeologists and historians, these images are among the most important sources of information about architectural styles and the development of architecture over time.

The words engraved on coins teach us about the languages spoken at the time and place they were created. A comparison of coins from a particular country over the years can provide evidence of conquests or upheavals in government through changes in the official language used on the coins. Similarly, the numbers imprinted on ancient coins give us valuable information about the numbering system of the country issuing the coins and how much the coins were worth at the time they were minted.

In addition, the quality of the coin itself tells us a lot about the technological prowess of the nation or society that made it, as evidenced by its ability to produce coinage at all and the types of metal it could smelt. Finally, the date on a coin tells us unequivocally not only when the civilization that made it was in power but also exactly when the rulers, heroes, buildings, and languages depicted on the coins were deemed important to that civilization.

Statements like these, however, have not stopped the criticism, particularly from those who decry some of Clifford's methods, including the practice of blasting pits with his propeller wash, which critics claim is not only environmentally harmful but seriously disturbs the integrity of an archaeological site.

Still, Clifford remains confident that what he is doing is highly beneficial in the search for the past. And, in addition to the ongoing excavation of the *Whydah*, he continues to search for treasure and history around the world.

In May 2014, Clifford caused a worldwide sensation by announcing that he had found off the coast of Haiti the wreck of the *Santa Maria*, the vessel that had served as Christopher Columbus's flagship during his epochal voyage to the New World. It was subsequently proven, however, that the sunken ship was actually a Spanish galleon from a later period.

Barry Clifford is only one of thousands of treasure hunters and marine archaeologists who, aided by ever more sophisticated deep-sea discovery and excavation equipment, are recovering artifacts from shipwrecks that took place as long ago as 1330 BCE. The science of marine archaeology was born in 1960 when a team off the coast of Cape Gelidonya in Turkey demonstrated that they could excavate a shipwreck underwater with the same scientific integrity and effectiveness as their counterparts working on land.

Archaeologists and divers are still probing that site, where artifacts from an ancient sunken merchant vessel from either Greece or Syria continue to enhance our understanding of ships' construction and commerce in the late Bronze Age.

Marine archaeologists carry out their work even in the frozen Arctic, where a team of Canadian archaeologists, scientists, and surveyors recently made two vital discoveries. In 2010 they found the British HMS *Investigator*, the ship that in 1850 discovered the long-sought-after Northwest Passage. Then, in 2014, they found the wreck of the HMS *Erebus*, one of the two ships that carried John Franklin and his 129-man crew on an earlier search for the Passage, a doomed expedition that resulted in the disappearance of the entire party. Artifacts from that wreck have provided important clues to solving the mystery of Franklin and his men.

The hundreds of excavations taking place continually beneath the world's seas challenge our imaginations and our spirits. They represent some of humankind's boldest achievements. They offer us dramatic proof that the vast ocean floor is, without question, the world's greatest museum.

A diver uses a state-of-the-art underwater video camera to record such vital information as the location of a shipwreck, items that have been discovered, and sites of possible future finds.

Source Notes

Introduction

p. 2: "the pyramids of the deep": quoted in Daniel Golden, "Raiders of the Lost Ark Salvage Firms Are Cleaning Out Davy Jones' Locker," *Boston Globe*, August 2, 1987.

p. 2: "I think there's more history . . . the world combined": quoted in "Mysteries of the Deep," *Scientific American Frontiers*, Chedd Angier/PBS, November 26, 2002.

Chapter One: The Slave Ship Whydah

p. 4: "made havoc . . . pesos in ransom": quoted in Earle, p. 87.

p. 5: records from the Royal African Company: Clifford and Kinkor, p. 23.

p. 10: "It would be needless . . . horror and slavery": Cugoano, p. 12.

Chapter Two: A New Pirate King

p. 15: "The truth about . . . in speculation": Clifford and Perry, p. 6.

p. 15: "I would not . . . dreams of Spanish gold": Vanderbilt, p. x.

pp. 16–17: "This flag . . . new men": quoted in Clifford and Perry, p. 7.

pp. 20–22: "I. Every man shall . . . by favour only": quoted in Vanderbilt, pp. 18–19.

p. 24: "a period . . . on the high seas": Candice Mallard, "Pirates of the Caribbean," *New York Times*, June 3, 2007.

p. 25: "put a Rope . . . almost dead": quoted in Botting, p. 60.

p. 25: "maniac and a brute": quoted in Pirate Biography, New England Pirate Museum, www.piratemuseum.com/edbiogra.htm.

Chapter Three: Bigger Ships, Bigger Prizes

p. 37: "The Money taken . . . Men on Board": quoted in Vanderbilt, p. 86.

p. 37: "'would first shoot . . . at the Mast'": ibid., p. 26.

Chapter Four: The Pirate Ship Whydah

pp. 40–41: "Many would have seen . . . against social grievances": quoted in Jose Martinez, "Controversial Ship Used in Slave Trade, Carried Black Pirates," *Telegraph* (Nashua, NH), November 22, 1993.

p. 41: "a subculture . . . spirit of revolt": quoted in Donovan Webster, "Pirates of the *Whydah*," *National Geographic*, May 1999.

p. 42: "War is . . . with pirates": quoted in Vanderbilt, p. 21.

p. 45: "an Indian born at Cape Codd": ibid., p. 41.

p. 47: "It's the story . . . were treated equally": quoted in Lisa Cornwell, "Pirates, the
Reality: Loot from the *Whydah*," *Washington Post,* July 3, 2007.

p. 48: "many a peg leg . . . culinary arts": Botting, p. 51.

p. 49: "In an honest . . . be my motto": quoted in Vanderbilt, p. 15.

Chapter Five: The Whydah *Rules the Waves*

p. 50: "away for the Capes . . . in company": quoted in Vanderbilt, p. 31.

pp. 50–51: The storm . . . the winds: Defoe, pp. 585–586.

p. 53: "with Rum . . . European Goods" and "the greatest part . . . on board their Ship":
quoted in Vanderbilt, p. 35.

p. 55: "cut away . . . destroyed her": quoted in Vanderbilt, p. 35.

p. 57: "You dog! . . . that inch too!": quoted in Botting, p. 57.

p. 59: "I'm sorry . . . sink her": quoted in Clifford and Turchi, p. 25.

p. 59: "Surely you . . . fellow thieves": ibid.

pp. 59–60: "Damn you . . . for employment?": ibid.

p. 60: "I cannot break . . . hand of God": ibid.

p. 60: "You are a devilish rascal . . . conscience tells me": ibid.

Chapter Six: The Wreck of the Whydah

p. 64: "laden with Tobacco, hides and other things": quoted in Vanderbilt, p. 41.

p. 64: "very well": ibid.

p. 65: "the inhabitants hear . . . round their hearths": Henry David Thoreau, "The
Highland Light," *Atlantic Monthly,* December 1864, p. 144.

p. 68: "Blasphemies, oaths, and horrid imprecations": Defoe, p. 586.

p. 71: "Ship ashore! All hands perishing!": Burbank, p. 1.

p. 74: "We pray Thee . . . the inhabitants": quoted in Lawrence, p. 193.

Chapter Seven: The Survivors

p. 77: "damn'd the Vessel . . . never seen her": quoted in Vanderbilt, p. 40.

p. 82: "So it is . . . Piracy and Robbery": quoted in Vanderbilt, p. 89.

pp. 82–83: "That such Persons . . . put to Death": ibid.

p. 83: "Treason, Oppression . . . Theft," "in remote . . . nor Relief," and "the Prisoners
      are all . . . Guilty": ibid., p. 90.

p. 83: "all Armed . . . taken Command": ibid., p. 91.

p. 83: "some Cloaths . . . Ship's Company": ibid.

p. 83: "if he would not find Liquor": ibid.

p. 85: "almost every hour . . . the condemned": Gosse, p. 209.

p. 85: "The struggle . . . display of his corpse": Hall, p. 14.

p. 85: "Thus we see . . . for the Future": Defoe, p. x.

p. 86: "forced no Body to go with them," "would take no Body against their Wills,"
      "declared himself to be now a Pirate," and "went up and . . . pyrates": ibid., p. 92

p. 86: "what they had to say for themselves": quoted in Vanderbilt, p. 92.

p. 86: "he attempted to . . . Spanish Town" and "the Governour . . . destroy the Town":
      ibid., p. 93.

p. 87: "threatened to . . . nothing to support him": ibid.

p. 87: "they would kill him . . . Unlawful Designs": ibid.

p. 87: "unavoidably forced to . . . among the Pyrates": ibid.

pp. 87–88: "Their pretence . . . liberty of Sinning" and "That [the accused] . . . plain
      and obvious": ibid., p. 94.

p. 88: "The Court . . . on your Souls": ibid., pp. 95–96.

p. 88: "compelled . . . join with the Pirates": ibid, p. 95.

p. 89: "the Execution of these Miserables": ibid., p. 105.

p. 91: "Behold, the End of Piracy": ibid., p. 112.

Chapter Eight: The Adventures of Cyprian Southack

p. 92: "The Pyrate Ship . . . cast away": quoted in Vanderbilt, p. 58.

p. 94: "Money, Bullion . . . the said Ship": *Boston News-Letter*, May 4, 1717.

p. 95: "Pirritt Rack": quoted in Vanderbilt, p. 63.

p. 99: "there had been . . . came ashoar": ibid., p. 64.

pp. 99–100: "go into any . . . door, chests, trunks": quoted in Snow, *True Tales*, p. 52.

p. 100: "Whereas there is . . . utmost peril": quoted in Vanderbilt, p. 70.

p. 102: "I am in . . . fish for [it]": ibid., p. 73.

p. 102: "a great sea" and "do nothing as yet": quoted in Barry and Turchi, p. 64.

pp. 102–103: "Monday, May 6 . . . on the Wreck": Vanderbilt, p. 73.

Chapter Nine: Legends

p. 105: "For many years . . . constantly wore": Thoreau, pp. 68–69.

pp. 109, 112: "Diver Jack Poole . . . to pieces": Snow, *True Tales*, p. 59.

p. 111: "Why make victims . . . thrown them overboard.": Minster.

p. 112: "It will be . . . of Wellfleet": quoted in Vanderbilt, p. 124.

Chapter Ten: The Search for the Whydah

p. 113: "When I was . . . about my feet": Vanderbilt, p. ix.

p. 114: "He told us . . . get to it": quoted in ibid., p. 127.

pp. 114, 116: "At 5 . . . from the wreck": ibid., p. 130.

p. 116: "3 miles . . . to Billingsgate": ibid.

p. 118: "That optimism . . . dive a shipwreck?": ibid., p. 136.

p. 118: "When I told . . . with a Kennedy?'": Clifford and Perry, p. 124.

p. 120: "our ability . . . our imaginations": "Technology: Observing Systems and Sensors," National Oceanic and Atmospheric Administration Ocean Explorer website, http://oceanexplorer.noaa.gov/technology/tools/tools.html.

p. 124: "The suite of tools . . . of yesteryear": "Modern Expeditions," NOAA Photo Library, http://www.photolib.noaa.gov/nurp/mod_expeditions.html.

p. 126: "very fine barrel . . . glass": Aristotle's *Problemata* quoted in Michael Lahanas, "Alexander the Great and the Bathysphere," http://www.mlahanas.de/Greeks/UnderWater.htm.

p. 128: "I think it's a small cannon": quoted in Clifford and Perry, p. 127.

p. 128: "Throw it back! That's a bomb!": ibid.

p. 128: "that first, terribly dry season . . . right place": Clifford and Perry, p. 126.

Chapter Eleven: Victory at Last

p. 130: "was young . . . this hole, too": Clifford and Perry, p. 143.

p. 130: "Hey, you guys! . . . cannons down there!": quoted in ibid.

p. 132: "toe prints still in the leather": quoted in Vanderbilt, p. 144.

p. 132: "At first . . . a date: 1684": ibid., p. 143.

p. 132: "This artifact . . . of the *Whydah*": Clifford and Perry, p. 146.

p. 133: "Imagine the sound . . . counted them": quoted in Vanderbilt, p. 147.

p. 133: "If we dug seven . . . scratched the surface": ibid., p. 148.

p. 135: "It's an early . . . wrecks out there": quoted in Clifford and Perry, p. 107.

p. 136: "There's something . . . tell what it is," "Maybe it's . . . don't recognize it," and "I don't think . . . a bell": ibid., p. 186.

p. 136: "My heart began . . . ship it was from": ibid., p. 187.

p. 136: "It looks like . . . from the *Whydah*": ibid., p. 188.

p. 137: "I tried not . . . damaging an artifact": ibid.

p. 138: "I don't think you could hope for more": quoted in Matthew Wald, "Bell Confirms that Salvors Found Pirate Ship of Legend," *New York Times,* November 1, 1985.

pp. 138, 143: "I guess I'll . . . stationery," "Not to mention . . . caps," and "Forget . . . change my tattoo": quoted in Clifford and Perry, p. 188.

p. 143: "Look at these . . . human lives": quoted in Donovan Webster, "Pirates of the *Whydah,*" *National Geographic,* May 1999.

p. 143: "On July 19 . . . pirates to exist": Clifford and Perry, p. 295.

p. 145: "To think . . . how can we stop?": ibid., p, 307.

Chapter Twelve: What the Artifacts Tell Us

p. 146: "Each shipwreck is . . . April 26, 1717": Clifford and Kinkor, p. 10.

p. 149: "thuggish white men with sabers": Donovan Webster, "Pirates of the *Whydah,*" *National Geographic,* May 1999.

p. 152: "In twenty minutes . . . tell me": Clifford and Perry, p. 149.

p. 152: "I had been looking . . . back then": quoted in Michael Levenson, "Remains Are Identified As a Boy Pirate," *Boston Globe,* June 2, 2006, p. B1.

p. 153: "I [am] not . . . as a historian": Clifford and Kinkor, p. 163.

p. 154: "newspapers in metal": "Newspapers in Metal: What Ancient Coins Tell Us," Simon Fraser University Continuing Education website, http://www.sfu.ca /continuing-studies/courses/ahcp/2014/09/ancient-coins/.

p. 154: "miniature libraries of history": "Ancient Secrets: Civilizations Revealed Through Coins," Simon Fraser University Continuing Education website, https://www.sfu.ca/continuing-studies/courses/scfc/2011/civilzations-revealed -through-coins/.

Bibliography

Bass, George F. *Archaeology Beneath the Sea*. New York: Walker, 1975.

Bolster, W. Jeffrey. *Black Jacks: African American Seamen in the Age of Sail*. Cambridge, MA: Harvard University Press, 1998.

Botting, Douglas. *The Pirates*. Alexandria, VA: Time-Life Books, 1978.

Burbank, Theodore Parker. *Cape Cod Shipwrecks: Graveyard of the Atlantic*. Millis, MA: Salty Pilgrim Press, 2013.

Clifford, Barry, and Kenneth J. Kinkor with Sharon Simpson. *Real Pirates: The Untold Story of the* Whydah *from Slave Ship to Pirate Ship*. Washington, DC: National Geographic, 2007.

Clifford, Barry, with Paul Perry. *Expedition Whydah: The Story of the World's First Excavation of a Pirate Treasure Ship and the Man Who Found Her*. New York: HarperCollins, 1999.

Clifford, Barry, with Peter Turchi. *The Pirate Prince: Discovering the Priceless Treasures of the Sunken Ship* Whydah. New York: Simon and Schuster, 1993.

Cordingly, David. *Under the Black Flag: The Romance and the Reality of Life Among the Pirates*. New York: Random House, 2006.

Cugoano, Quobna Ottobah. *Thoughts and Sentiments on the Evil of Slavery*. 1787. Reprint edited and with an introduction by Vincent Carretta, New York: Penguin, 1999.

Defoe, Daniel. *A General History of the Pyrates*. 1724. Reprint, Mineola, NY: Dover, 1972.

Earle, Peter. *The Sack of Panamá: Captain Morgan and the Battle for the Caribbean*. New York: St. Martin's, 2007.

Ellms, Charles. *The Pirates Own Book: Authentic Narratives of the Most Celebrated Sea Robbers*. 1837. Reprint edited by David W. Whitehead, New York: Dover, 2003.

Gosse, Philip. *The History of Piracy*. New York: Dover, 2007.

Hall, Andrew H. "*The Last Days of Pirates*." PhD diss., Vanderbilt University, 1998. https://discoverarchive.vanderbilt.edu/bitstream/handle/1803/177/98HHTHallAH.pdf?sequence=1.

Jameson, J. F. *Privateering and Piracy in the Colonial Period.* New York: Augustus M. Kelly, 1970.

Lawrence, Iain. *The Wreckers.* New York: Random House, 1999.

Mathewson, R. Duncan. *Treasure of the* Atocha: *A Four Hundred Million Dollar Archaeological Adventure.* Foreword by Mel Fisher. New York: Dutton, 1986.

Merchant, Jo. *Decoding the Heavens: A 2,000-Year-Old Computer—and the Century-Long Search to Discover Its Secrets.* Boston: Da Capo, 2011.

Minster, Christopher. "Pirates: Truth, Facts, Legends, and Myths." http://latinamericanhistory.about.com/od/TheGoldenAgeofPiracy1700-1725/p/Pirates-Truth-Facts-Legends-And-Myths.htm

Middlekauff, Robert. *The Mathers: Three Generations of Puritan Intellectuals, 1596–1728.* New York: Oxford University Press, 1977.

Pringle, Patrick. *Jolly Roger: The Story of the Great Age of Piracy.* New York: Dover, 2001.

Rankin, Hugh F. *The Golden Age of Piracy.* New York: Holt, Rinehart and Winston, 1969.

Reynard, Elizabeth. *The Narrow Land: Folk Chronicles of Old Cape Cod.* Boston: Houghton Mifflin, 1978.

Snow, Edward Rowe. *Great Storms and Famous Shipwrecks of the New England Coast.* Boston: Yankee Publishing, 1943.

———. *True Tales of Buried Treasure.* New York: Dodd, Mead, 1960.

Stevenson, Robert Louis. *Treasure Island.* 1905. Reprint, New York: Dover, 1993.

Thomas, Hugh. *The Slave Trade: The Story of the Atlantic Slave Trade; 1440–1870.* New York: Simon and Schuster, 1999.

Thoreau, Henry David. *Cape Cod.* 1849–1857. Reprint, New York: Empire Books, 2013.

Vanderbilt, Arthur T. *Treasure Wreck: The Fortune and Fate of the Pirate Ship* Whydah. Boston: Houghton Mifflin, 1986.

Photography Credits

p. 6: Development Education Centre, South Yorkshire, England • p. 10: Library of Congress • p. 18: Library of Congress • p. 30: Library of Congress • p. 35: Library of Congress • p. 54: Library of Congress • p. 66: Collection of the author • p. 71: Alamy Photo Archive • p. 72: Library of Congress • p. 81: Library of Congress • p. 90: Massachusetts Historical Society • p. 93: Library of Congress • p. 98: Library of Congress • p. 101: Archives of the Commonwealth of Massachusetts • p. 115: Library of Congress • p. 117: Courtesy of National Geographic Creative • p. 121: Courtesy of National Geographic Creative • p. 125: National Oceanic and Atmospheric Administration • p. 131: Courtesy of National Geographic Creative • p. 134: Courtesy of National Geographic Creative • p. 139: Courtesy of National Geographic Creative • p. 141: National Archives • p. 144: Courtesy of National Geographic Creative • p. 147: Courtesy of National Geographic Creative • p. 150: Courtesy of National Geographic Creative • p. 155: Courtesy of National Geographic Creative • p. 159: National Oceanic and Atmospheric Administration

Acknowledgments

I am most grateful to Rachel Smith for the inspired design she has brought to this book. And I owe a huge debt of gratitude to Pamela Marshall for the meticulous way every fact and quotation was checked and authenticated. Thanks also to Miriam Newman, Jennifer McFadden, Linda Rizkalla, Rebecca Demont, and Emily Quinan for their much appreciated contributions. Finally, once again—thank you, Hilary Van Dusen, a true daughter of the sea, for recognizing the magic in this story, for sharing so fully in my bringing it to life, and for once again keeping me on the straight and narrow—never an easy task.

Index

Note: page numbers in italics indicate images